CO-PARENTING
within
COERCIVE CONTROL

A Parent's Guide to Helping and Supporting their Children

Including 31 important reminders for children

LIS HOYTE

Copyright © 2022 Lis Hoyte

Co-parenting within Coercive Control:
A Parent's Guide to Helping and Supporting their Children

All rights reserved.

No part of this publication may be reproduced, distributed, or transmitted in any form or by any means, including photocopying, recording, or other electronic or mechanical methods, without the prior written permission of the publisher, except in the case of brief quotations embodied in critical reviews and certain other non-commercial uses permitted by copyright law.

Tarnya Coley

Printed in the United Kingdom
First Printing 2022
First Edition 2022

978-1-7391921-0-5

Disclaimer

Although the author has made every effort to ensure that the information in this book was correct at press time and while this publication is designed to provide accurate information in regard to the subject matter covered, the author assumes no responsibility for errors, inaccuracies, omissions, or any other inconsistencies herein and hereby disclaim any liability to any party for any loss, damage, or disruption caused by errors or omissions, whether such errors or omissions result from negligence, accident, or any other cause. Throughout the book fictional names have been used.

The author is not providing anything that could constitute therapeutic, legal or other specialist advice. The services of a competent professional should be sought. Always seek professional advice This publication is meant as a source of valuable information for the reader, however it is not meant as a substitute for direct expert assistance. If such level of assistance is required contact the National Domestic Abuse Helpline- https://www.nationaldahelpline.org.uk or https://mensadviceline.org.uk/

Table of Contents

Acknowledgments 5

Who this guide is for and how to use it. 7

Introduction for Parents 11

Dealing with Professionals – The Conflict 15

Associations with the Coercive Controller 18

Ways Children May Behave Within Coercive Control. 21

Conversation starters. 24

Helpful things children may say to feel empowered 26

A Message to Your Child – Part 1. 46

Important Reminders for Children 47

A Message to Your Child – Part 2. 83

Final Word to Parents 84

Review Ask 85

Craving more? 86

About the Author 87

Acknowledgments

Thank you to all my clients, both women and men from all types of relationship categorisations, that spoke from the heart to make this parenting guide possible.

Thank you for your consent and how amazing you have been in making this guide possible. You have been incredible; the courage and positive stance taken by all involved speaks volumes about the love you have for your children. I appreciate you all.

Thank you to Marc Lowe for always standing by my side and being my biggest supporter. As a family, we are truly blessed to have you in our lives.

Who this guide is for and how to use it

It is important to understand that this help guide is for parents who are co-parenting within coercive control. We hold many ideologies that abuse must include physical violence. Coercive control, however, is a separate type of abuse, and it goes far beyond the physical. Luke and Ryan Harts lived experience of coercive control cements this, in that they did not experience physical violence at the hands of their father.

This guide is intended to be used in supporting parents and children with conversations that children may struggle to navigate through. When I use the word "parent", I refer to parents in every type of relationship in terms of intersectionality. Coercive control does not discriminate, and many clients that I have worked with from the LGBT community have expressed their challenges within coercive control from all levels of the justice system – reporting and accessing support has its own separate struggles. Their opinions have been very much a part of this guide. The help, support, and guidance from clients has been phenomenal in the creation of this guide. I wanted to produce something that parents and children could relate to, such as other people's experiences within coercive control, the patterns and manipulation tactics used on children, the fact that coercive control is very much a reality, and finally, that I am not alone.

The scenarios featured are aimed at helping children understand how they can respond to someone who is coercive and controlling in their behaviour, should they wish to, if they feel confident enough in doing so, and more importantly, if you feel it is safe for your children to do so. Reading through the scenarios with your child will help you both to feel that there are other ways of responding to abusive people than to retaliate in kind. This will just fuel them further and ultimately allow them to use it against you.

Children experience coercive control (the foundation of most domestic abuse) on many different levels. It is my belief that children do not feel comfortable or desire to be involved in such experiences. However, you can be assured that the controlling parent will bring the child into this arena in various ways. These can include parental alienation, controlling the child emotionally and financially, grooming, and gaslighting. This list is not exhaustive.

I have debated with many, and will continue to, regarding how much children should be aware of within coercive control – how much we should be discussing with our children to protect them. However, it is my belief that children should be equipped with the tools to defend and empower themselves when experiencing coercive control. Whilst I am not here to force beliefs or challenge anyone's moral compass, I believe it is more detrimental to the child experiencing coercive control if they are unequipped to respond – children should at least be aware of what is happening to them on an abusive level.

Children need to feel that their voices are being heard. The more tools we give them, the more they will be empowered to say how they feel about how they are being treated and what happens to them when they are without the protection of a parent who isn't coercive and controlling.

Within this guide, support has been offered to parents who are struggling with their child's behaviour in the context of how they treat the parent that is being coercively controlled, and how they treat and react to other siblings that are being coercive controlled. I have laid out the foundations of how a child may behave by referring to these as 'Types of Behaviour Expressed'. I specifically added this section for three reasons based on concerns my clients had around their children's behaviour, particularly when the parent relationships were ending, and everyone was still residing together, however, the same behaviours continued and escalated further within the post-separation stage.

Secondly, to help people understand that some of the behaviours children display are a direct result of trying to protect their own hearts. At times, this behaviour towards the protective parent can seem unjust, unfair, and worrying to the protective parent. And finally, because it wasn't until one of my own children came to me and expressed their feelings that I truly began to understand the dynamics of their behaviour to appease the coercive controller and to protect their own heart.

The child responses within the scenarios may come across to some as too advanced – I offer the following explanation here. There have been many occasions where fathers have sent their children (boys or girls as young as six years old) photographs via their mobile phones of known rapists and paedophiles, with messages attached stating that their mother is having a relationship with these perpetrators, and that the police are involved. This is something that occurs regularly and is so damaging that it instils fear in children, bringing about doubt in the child's mind towards the protective mother/parent. That is why it is my belief that these responses will enable children to respond appropriately when met with such adult themes. Spreading awareness of coercive control accompanied with some tools, is a hopeful starting place in protecting the emotional and psychological abuse endured by children via coercive control.

Everything in this guide has been written from experience: either something that I have directly experienced, or that my clients have experienced, shared with their consent.

The names given to support the scenarios below are not attributed to me or any of my clients – they are fictional. I have used both "Mum" and "Dad" in each scenario so as not to discriminate, however it is important to remember that all scenarios have come from different types of relationships. For this guide, my clients and I decided to use "Mum" and "Dad" to aid understanding for smaller children. Some of the scenarios are focused on the negative side of "Dad" for three reasons: the inclusion of male coercive control victims in their homosexual relationships; coercive control being predominantly a male perpetrated form of domestic abuse against females; and finally, comparing my client base of males and females within coercive control, the number is significantly higher for females experiencing coercive control from males.

I have intended for each of the scenarios and illustrations to provide a visual to help children understand and resonate with some typical behaviours they may experience within abuse.

Towards the end of the book, there are 31 important reminders for children to use – one for every day of the month to assist with mindset through repetition to help them feel empowered and gain self-confidence. The conclusion is particularly important and written especially for children. Reading this section with your child and supporting them with anything they may not understand will be rewarding.

I do not claim to have all the answers, or that my tools have a sure-fire way of working, but what I can say is that it has helped my children find a little relief – a little empowerment. This guide is giving you something that I never had, or even had the energy to search for to help myself at that time. We all need a little help sometimes, especially when new tactics come into play that are used by the coercive controller.

I am still an advocate and continue to work on programmes to help and support perpetrators of coercive control to better understand how their behaviour affects others close to them. As coercive control does not discriminate, programmes should reflect different types of relationships, cultures, and races. Let's just say that this guide is a little gift from me to you – the protective parent.

Introduction for Parents

You have probably said far too many "*Really?*"s and "*What?*"s in response to the disbelief about the challenges faced while co-parenting within coercive control. Based on this, I want to say to you, congratulations. Yes, congratulations for getting through some of the things that you may have experienced. Congratulations for breaking free from coercive control: it is one of the hardest abusive relationships to set yourself free from, due to its complexities. Congratulations for being resilient to the smear campaign. Well done for soldiering on when the coercive controller attempted (perhaps successfully) to control the narrative that others believed about you. Well done for keeping sane if your reputation has been tarnished, along with everything that you stand for. Well done for battling through the frustration of being open and honest, to then be subjected to, and dismissed via tactics of DARVO (deny, attack, and reverse victim and offender – the easiest escape to being held accountable). Well done and congratulations for holding on to your truth that had been devalued.

Whilst I appreciate you may not feel worthy of any "*Well done*'s or "*Congratulation*'s yet, believe me, you will get there. You will feel an overwhelming sense of pride when such a paradigm shift occurs, especially because you would have created it to protect your children.

Based on this, you are one of the strongest human beings ever – this is something that you should keep reminding yourself.

Those of you who read my first publication, "Break Free: A Transformational Journey and Paradigm Shift out of Coercive Control", will be aware that I intended to write a children's book entitled, "Some Awesome Things Kiddies Can Say to Feel Empowered".

The title and subject matter have been revised in this publication to reflect the issues that real people face within coercive control, both protective parents and children, to give more in-depth explanations of what children are going through. It will inform parents at a greater level to navigate the complexities of co-parenting within coercive control.

The intention of writing this second publication has been the direct result of experiencing the complexities of being in a coercive and controlling relationship myself. Since leaving my abusive relationship back in 2019 after 18 years, writing this guide brings together many parents' continued struggles of breaking free from coercive control when children are involved, which brings to light the difficulties of post- separation abuse where children are used to enable the coercive controller to maintain control over the protective parent and the children involved. The problem here is that these abusive behaviours can be very difficult to detect if you are not accustomed to or have not experienced dealing with such behaviours. No evidence does not mean you are lying or you weren't abused. Continue to speak your truth.

Another reason for writing this publication, which I also touched upon in "Break Free", is that my children were going through a challenging time wanting and needing answers for what they were seeing and experiencing. I couldn't find the words to explain to them due to my own anger and resentment about what was happening to them.

As a result, I just said nothing because I didn't have the skills to explain what I wanted to say. The anger I was feeling inside, I now believe, would have impacted their behaviour in a negative way where they would have been unable to process or make sense of what they were involved in. However, to their detriment and my own, I saw that this wasn't the right decision and my children suffered in this respect. They suffered from the very thing I was trying to protect them from: not being honest about what was happening in their lives. This didn't serve anyone involved well – including the other parent.

I believe that children, while not needing to know all the details of an abusive parent's behaviour, should be equipped to respond when abusive things are said to them, or unfair expectations are placed upon them.

We must all bear in mind that emotional and psychological abuse is when an adult makes a choice to leave invisible scars on children. It is our duty, as protective parents, to be aware of the damaging effects this type of abuse has on children.

The issues that many people experience currently are exacerbated by the law at all levels – from the initial phone calls to social services, to how these telephone conversations play out, reporting psychological and emotional abuse, reporting abuse to the police and the complexities of burden of proof within coercive control. Coercive control can affect the lives of children, their relationships with others, and ultimately who they choose as partners and friendship groups in their lives.

Let's protect our beautiful-souled children from a distance to the best of our ability by at least providing them with some tools. It is not our duty to control our children but to accept that they, too, are emotional, vibrational beings who need to be respected, understood, and guided.

When it comes to supporting children within domestic abuse situations, it is important to understand that any abuse that a child has had to endure is not their fault. Some professionals that work closely with children hold the belief that in some circumstances it is somehow the child's fault that leads them to be abused, perhaps due to them behaving in a certain way. They believe that if a child would have adapted their behaviour, the abuse would not have occurred. This mindset is extremely dangerous as no child is ever deserving of abuse. This can be particularly distressing, especially when protective parents reach out for help and support from professionals.

The next chapter will present some areas of concern that parents and children experience within coercive control and why trusting your instincts is so important.

Dealing with Professionals – The Conflict

The above heading is a tricky one which extends to the support available to children and protective parents within any type of abusive relationship.

I will begin with some important statements:

When protective parents reach out for help and support within coercive control and are met with resistance, it leaves parents feeling 'helpless'.

When protective parents reach out to the police for help and support within coercive control and are met with resistance, it leaves parents feeling 'let down'.

When protective parents reach out for help and support to gain funds for legal representation which are unavailable, it leaves parents feeling 'trapped'.

When protective parents run out of funds or are unable to afford solicitor fees to get things in place to support and protect their children, it leaves parents feeling 'frustrated'.

It may appear that the above statements are just focusing on the negative, but I like to think about it in terms of spreading awareness of coercive control in its entirety to enable professionals and the system to adjust policies and practices to reflect the nature of this type of abuse. What I can say is, it becomes soul-destroying when those experiencing coercive control are told by professionals that they are unable to help and support in the correct way due to lack of knowledge and/or training on coercive control. It may be a consideration for those central to coercive control and working in the domestic abuse support arena to take on board the struggles of their employees and work in unity to find a process where police officers, social workers and early help teams etc. work with those who have experienced coercive control to help to spot the signs, know the manipulation tactics and develop the ability to check areas that may have been missed. It may help to develop strategies on how to engage in the processes of adequate questioning of perpetrators, deeper knowledge on historical events findings and the importance of these within cases of coercive control. If victims of coercive control implement training from their experience, this would be invaluable.

Nevertheless, the new Domestic Abuse Act 2021 and its statutory guidelines make some amazing changes around coercive control. It is the first Domestic Abuse Act that includes children as victims, which shows a positive move forward. However, it is important to note that no law, policy, practice, or procedure is credible if the professionals involved within these roles are ill-equipped to deal with coercive control or to identify the most important signs to even begin the process of accessing the correct support and advice to give to those experiencing coercive control.

Other factors involved when dealing with some professionals who have little or no experience of dealing with coercive control is that they tend to give advice to parents that is unrealistic in nature when it comes to co-parenting with someone who is coercive controlling. Here, it is understandable why certain states in America are considering wiping out the mediation process within coercive control purely because this expectation places additional demands on and use of the system to further control victims of coercive control.

All professionals must focus on their part in helping children to work through their lived experiences instead of placing unrealistic expectations on protective parents while co- parenting within coercive control.

As a society, I believe that too many protective parents, mainly mothers, are ending up homeless with their children due to coercive control, without finances and adequate support to look after or even feed their children. As a society, more needs to be done – more help and support with the rising costs of energy prices, and financial support for legal aid and representation for those experiencing coercive control.

The most important message to take from here is that *you* know your children best, not the professional, not the coercive controller, *you* as the protective parent. Always ask questions and always challenge if something doesn't feel right.

Associations with the Coercive Controller

It has become apparent to me that children tend not to be believed nor are they deemed worthy of being listened to when they disclose that they are experiencing abuse – this has detrimental effects on children.

I appreciate that not everyone will confront someone they know is abusive and that certainly isn't the expectation here. However, when a child discloses to a trusted adult about how abusive an adult has been to them, I can assure you, it would have taken a lot for a child to have done this. They would have entrusted you with some of the most hurtful things that have happened to them. My clients have detailed that it is one of the most hurtful things when children ask, "Why is that person still speaking to them [the abuser]?" It further confuses them. They may question whether what they are experiencing is abuse at all. Otherwise, why would someone known to the child continue to have a relationship with those they know have abused the children? This is especially when the children have taken it upon themselves to disclose things to the person in question but then see that person socialising with their abuser.

In attempts to ease the anger and anxiety of my clients, I have spent a considerable amount of time trying to find explanations as to why associations with the abuser may still occur after a child discloses to a trusted adult. The truth is that people use many justifications, but this area isn't one that can be controlled, unfortunately. You can never control how someone else behaves whether you agree or not: as hard as it is, you must focus only on what you can control. I do believe, however, that this reality is something we all need to be aware of. That little conversation that the child has seen the trusted person having with the coercive controller cements hurt and pain in their heart, while the trusted person may not have even given it a second thought and may justify their continued relationships with the coercive controller "for the sake of the child".

We must all come together to set in motion a new consciousness of how we define, act upon, perceive, and interpret coercive control and how it affects the child's life.

It is equally important to understand what our own behaviours are showing. When you side with their abuser, you are agreeing with the abuser continuing to harm children. The more the child heals, the more they will be aware of who plays a part via their silence.

Children need non-abusive adults in their lives. Please, let's remember that child abuse is about power, control, and coercion that harmful people exert over children. It reflects the abuser's inability to respect children, care for and honour their innocence as smaller human beings.

Where our focus goes, energy flows, which is why these simple tools can help children be aware of some of the tactics used against them that are often hard to see. Abusive parents are skilled manipulators. Children need help and support, not just because of this but because the children also love these skilled manipulations: they enjoy gifts, holidays, treats, and being given full reign of what they may choose. This makes the abuse even more insidious. In time, children will start to understand what they are going through and understand how they are feeling. They will work things out for themselves if they have the right support and guidance. You can't always be there and can't always control every situation that your child may encounter (especially until the existing laws can be implemented effectively to support children). Abuse is wrong and is a clear infringement of human rights.

In all that we do, please remember our actions give our children clear messages about what is acceptable and what is not acceptable in life. Please choose wisely, with your children always in mind. Be that protective parent no matter who else agrees with you or not.

By now, my desire to help and support children and parents co-parenting within coercive control should be evident. This has allowed me to look deeper into children's behaviour and why they react the way they do. This is part of helping parents understand the behaviour of children who may come across as extremely cold, negative, and unforgiving towards them. Knowing about, or at least being consciously aware of these behaviours, can soothe how parents feel when children become somewhat cold towards them. Bear in mind that there is an even bigger emotional roller coaster that many parents endure, which can be argued to be a separate abuse of the heart. This involves dealing with the complexities of their children's behaviour because of the coercive control they are witnessing and therefore subjected to.

The next section expands on areas that create great unrest to my clients and others experiencing coercive control and has been constructed to discuss the way some children may behave. I present it here to you in the hope that you may find a modicum of peace about the way your children may be behaving towards you.

Ways Children May Behave Within Coercive Control

Type of behaviour expressed – 1:
Join the dominant member.

Sometimes it is easier for children to side with their abuser. This is usually done out of fear or wanting to be accepted by meeting the unreasonable demands of their abuser. It is usually done to avoid being targeted. Even though it is extremely painful for the child to see others being targeted, it emphasises their need to be accepted and remain on the side of their abuser.

Type of behaviour expressed – 2:
Active participation in the abuse.

The difference from the first behaviour is that here the child becomes an active participant in the acts that the abuser carries out. For example, putting the protective parent down with insults. The child, regardless of age, will find their own way to justify this aggression towards their protective parent, and in many cases often aggressive towards their siblings.

Type of behaviour expressed – 3:
Angry and dismissive of the coercive controller.

Children are very sensitive human beings, so when they see things that are not fair, it breaks them at their core. When they experience injustices, especially when done to someone they love wholeheartedly, the child may be openly angry and confrontational with their abuser.

Type of behaviour expressed – 4:
Side with protective parent.

Though this can be very uncomfortable for the child, and the child can remain in a state of psychological warfare, their need to protect the protective parent far outweighs their fear of any consequences they could be subjected to.

Type of behaviour expressed – 5:
Become the mediator between the protective parent and coercive controller.

This can put considerable pressure on the child, as it involves careful planning and prediction of how others might behave. In this situation, it is the behaviour of the coercive controller that proves the most stressful for the child to deal with. This is draining physically, intellectually, emotionally, socially, psychologically, and behaviourally for the child.

Type of behaviour expressed – 6:
Total disengagement.

The child simply retreats into their own shell. They become a social recluse and are unable to process their lived experiences.

Type of behaviour expressed – 7:
Acting in a superior position to sibling.

Feeling guilt over being in a superior position to sibling.

Sometimes, within these types of relationships, the coercive controller may financially groom the better-behaved or more compliant sibling.

While the more compliant sibling is very aware that they are being given more and treated better, it still makes them feel uneasy. From the coercive controller's perspective, this is also a way to expose the other sibling's non-compliant behaviour in order to gain control of that non-compliant sibling.

Whilst on the surface this may read as a simple reward system – the way teachers and some parents may use a behavioural modification strategy – it is purely about power and control over a child's emotions through fear and manipulation.

With the above situations, it is important to be aware of the reasoning behind why some children may behave in these ways. Stand back and become the observer of your situation. Children are guided by how they feel more than adults, so in time, just gently remind them to trust their instincts. They will work out what feels right and wrong, but it takes time. In the meantime, here is a reminder for you: you cannot control what happens when you are not present, but you have everything inside of you to deal with situations that you experience.

Trust and focus on how you would like your relationship to "be" or "feel" with your child. Focus there – this is what you can control.

Conversation starters

Sometimes, it is difficult to start conversations with children and young people. I have found that it takes time for your children to feel comfortable telling you things that have gone on. Particularly when they themselves are confused by situations they find themselves in when you are not present.

It can be productive to let the child come to you on returning from time spent with the coercive controller, to speak to you about what may or may not have happened. It's important not to force anything. This may result in your child choosing not to mention anything for the sake of making life easier. Sometimes, when children return from an abusive household, they want to forget what has happened, so it may be a few days before your child feels willing to open up. The key is not to force them, but to allow them to express themselves when the time comes.

Many people take the stance that protective parents should not ask questions when children return from contact, in that it is a boundary that shouldn't be crossed. However, I am referring to conversations you may choose to have with your child, not questioning, especially if this comes across negatively. There is a clear difference. What is important to take on here is that it's not actually about what others believe to work for your child, it's about knowing your child and what works best for them.

With all conversation starters, it helps to remain neutral. People's ideas of right or wrong can vary somewhat. It's better to go down the road of what is moral to you.

This will determine how you want your children to be treated by anyone else in their life in the future. The key is to be within your own moral compass when starting these conversations. By doing this, you have a better chance of being the observer of your situation.

Try to avoid the questioning and asking specifics about which individuals were involved. Children may be reluctant to tell you if they believe it will hurt your feelings. Once children feel that you will be hurt by something, they may try not to upset you by withholding information that may need to be shared with you. If this happens, it can be very difficult for children to feel able to open up to you about other things that may have gone on. Going on walks with the child, remaining side by side, giving less eye contact or talking to the child while completing another activity can also be extremely helpful.

A good conversation starter may be

- What sort of activities did you get up to?
- Did you have your favourite meal again?

It only takes a simple conversation starter like this to encourage the flow of conversation.

Just remember, you know your child best regardless of what others may say or think… you've got this!

HELPFUL THINGS CHILDREN MAY SAY TO FEEL EMPOWERED

Scenarios and Children's responses

SCENARIO: MOBILE PHONE ISSUES

Scenario

Kaci has just witnessed an alcohol-fuelled fight in her home between her mum and stepdad. She is looking for her mobile phone but can't find it. Kaci asks her mum if she has seen it. Her mother asks why she needs it. Kaci replies that she needs to call her dad because she is feeling unsafe. Kaci's mum says, "You can only speak with your dad if you are sitting in front of us so we can hear you. If anything bad is said, you will be in big trouble."

Kaci goes to her room crying, scared, and afraid to make the call to her dad.

> **Child's response:** I should be able to call Dad if I feel unsafe. He is my dad. I am not meant to feel unsafe.

SCENARIO: ILLNESS

Scenario

Pierre is walking to school with his dad and his dad says, "Son, I've got something to tell you. I may die soon. I think it's best if you tell Mum that you want to live here with me full time as I'll be dead soon. It won't be fair if I don't spend my final days with you, will it?"

Child's response: Hearing about your illness and dying makes me upset. Can we either stop talking about this or speak about something positive please? I think I would struggle to live with you if you were going to be so ill.

SCENARIO:
HOSPITAL CONCERNS

Scenario

Toya is in the garden playing with a friend and falls over and bumps her head on the concrete. Her mum says to her, "It will be much better if you live here full time with me because there are more people here. If you have an accident like this at your dad's house, there may not be people around to make sure that you get to hospital in an emergency."

Child's response: Dad will always find a way to make sure I am ok. If I am ever in trouble, Dad will call the ambulance straight away. Dad loves me and will always cope.

SCENARIO:
TRYING TO CONTROL A CHILD'S FRIENDSHIPS

Scenario

Shona is picked up from school by her dad, who sees Shona saying goodbye to her friend. Shona's dad says, "I really don't like your friends. I think you should make some new friends because I have a feeling that girl will turn out just like her mother. It's time you made some new friends, anyway."

Child's response: My friends have always been my friends. I love them, and I have no reason not to keep my friends. They treat me well and they make me happy.

SCENARIO: CONTROLLING A CHILD'S EMOTIONS

Scenario

Marcus is in his room crying because he misses his mum. Marcus's dad pushes open his door and says, "You do know it's not fair if you don't cry for me at your mum's house. It makes me feel upset if you only cry for your mum. You are not to cry for your mum in this house ever again, ok?"

Child's response: I am not responsible for your feelings. This is how I feel and there is nothing wrong with that.

SCENARIO: CONTROL OVER A CHILD'S CLOTHING

Scenario

Darnell is at the shop with his mum when she says out of the blue, "It's important that I always choose your clothes for you because I know what you look nice in when others see you."

> **Child's response**: I would like to be able to choose some of my clothes as it's not about how others see me, it's about how comfortable I will feel.

SCENARIO:
I LOVE YOU MORE

Scenario

Torri's dad says to her, "I love you much more than your mum loves you."

Child's response: You have no way of knowing how much Mum loves me. I know Mum loves me and I love her. That's enough for me.

SCENARIO: GROOMING

Scenario

Jude's dad says to him, "You can have anything you want here. You know your mum hasn't got much money. If you cry and tell your mum you want to live with me full time, I can buy you whatever you want."

Child's response: I don't think it's fair or right that I don't see Mum anymore. I would rather see Mum than have gifts or money. I love my mum, and I would miss her.

SCENARIO:
POST SEPARATION CONTROL

What friends has dad had over? Show me around the house when we have our face time!!

Scenario

Kallie comes home from high school and her mum says to her, "You need to tell me what your dad gets up to. Who comes to the house? Are there any new female friends? Daddy is trying to stop you from seeing me, so it's important you give me this information because some women do horrible things to children, and I need to be able to protect you."

> **Child's response:** I'm a bit confused. I'm not allowed to mention to Dad anything that goes on here, so I don't know why you are asking me to do it to him. I don't think that's fair. I don't feel comfortable doing it. If you need to find out anything, that should be between adults. I don't want to be involved.

SCENARIO: SPEAKING NEGATIVELY OF OTHER PARENT. (PARENTAL ALIENATION)

Scenario

Jaden is sitting in his room, reading. His dad enters his room and says, "I'm really sorry, but your mum is being investigated by the police. She won't tell you the truth, but you have to believe me. She is a horrible person and has done some terrible things to me. Even her friends don't really like her, and the police know."

Child's response: When you say things like this to me, it makes me sad. This has nothing to do with me and it is for adults to sort out. Can you please stop talking to me about things like this?

SCENARIO: MAKING ARRANGEMENTS FOR THE CO-PARENTING HOUSEHOLD

Scenario

Shannon's mum wants her to go to trampolining class every week. Shannon's mum says that Shannon needs to say that she is sad to miss it so her dad can take her once a week, too. Shannon's mum says, "It's up to me what happens in Dad's house too because I'm in control, and Mummy's rules are still the most important."

> **Child's response:** Dad is not able to make these arrangements as he has other plans, and he can't be in two places at once. That trampolining class doesn't fit into my routine at Dad's house, but this has been explained to me. I'm fine with it and I won't be upset. I can see my friends at school.

SCENARIO: INTIMIDATION AND THREATS OF VIOLENCE

Scenario

Kanisha's dad says, "I'm sorry I smashed the plate on the floor next to you, but it wasn't my fault. You made me angry. You don't need to mention anything to Mum, I didn't actually hit you, so it doesn't matter. If Mum knows, she will be sad. You don't want to make her sad, do you?"

> **Child's response:** Thanks for being concerned about Mum, but if anyone does that to me, it's important for me to tell Mum.

SCENARIO: I PAID, SO YOU MUST...

Scenario

Conrad has two pairs of trainers. He chooses to wear the ones his mum has bought for him, as they are his favourites. Conrad's dad says, "I paid for the other trainers, so you must wear those ones – other people will think you look better in those ones."

> **Child's response:** Regardless of who bought them for me, focusing on what others think I look like means other people's opinions of me matter more. I don't think that's right.

SCENARIO: CONTROLLING EMOTIONS

Scenario

Bronage is sitting doing some writing. Her dad comes in intoxicated and wanting to dance with her. Her dad feels frustrated that Bronage wants to continue writing. He grabs the writing book from Bronage's hands, and it rips. Bronage cries. Her dad says, "You are so sensitive – stop crying now."

> **Child's response:** My emotions are my own, and if I cry or want to be quiet, there is nothing wrong with that. It is not my duty to make you happy.

SCENARIO: MATERIAL THINGS ARE BETTER (PUTTING DOWN OTHER PARENTS)

Scenario

Leon is walking into Sainsbury's with his dad and has a full view of all the cars in the car park. Leon's dad points out a car that is like his mum's car and says to Leon, "Can you ask your mum if she likes her car? It's rubbish and doesn't look very nice. I'm sure it's unsafe for her to be driving you around in it. My car is much better, don't you think?"

Child's response: Mum's car is all she could afford and it's safe for me. That's the most important thing. If you want to find out whether Mum likes her car, you can ask her. I don't want to be involved.

SCENARIO: KEEPING SECRETS AROUND BED WETTING

Scenario

Tyson is scared to go to bed at night due to hearing arguments and seeing fights at his mum's house. These arguments and fights cause Tyson worry and anxiety and as a result he wets the bed.

Tyson's mum says, "Make sure you keep wetting a secret: people will think you are baby if they find out. You know your dad will tell people. It's between us, ok?"

> **Child's response:** I will not be keeping any secrets from Dad because I don't think it's right or fair. He has a right to know, as it could be something he could help me with.

SCENARIO: ASSUMING AUTHORITY OVER PHYSICAL ABUSE

Scenario

Kerlese's dad found out that she told her mum that he pulled Kelese's arm violently and dragged her.

He says, "You must not tell anyone what I've done. It's ok I didn't hit you. I would never hurt you for no reason. You'll get me in trouble – you don't want that do you?"

> **Child's response:** I don't believe anyone should hurt me or have the right to hurt me. When you hurt me, it scares me. I will tell Mum if it happens again.

SCENARIO: JUSTIFYING TAKING CHILDREN AWAY ON TRIPS

Scenario

Joel is playing with his friends and his mum comes out and tells him she's booking a holiday. Joel asks if his dad knows. Joel's mum responds, "We don't need Daddy's permission. I can take you anywhere I want to if it's in this country."

Child's response: Dad would be worried if you took me without telling him. I think its best that I let Dad know, as this is not helping me to feel comfortable with going.

SCENARIO: PREPARING CHILDREN FOR WHAT TO SAY WHEN OUTSIDE AGENCIES BECOME INVOLVED

I will only speak my truth

Scenario

Chanel is playing when her dad comes into her bedroom and says, "Those people who came to see us were nice but it's important you only tell them nice things about being here, not the bad stuff, ok? You can order whatever you want from Amazon if you say nice things and don't get Daddy in trouble."

Child's response: I will only speak my truth about how I feel and what goes on here.

A Message to Your Child – Part 1

Hey, beautiful little human! Below are some important reminders that I have put together for you. You can say them as often as you like – whatever feels good to you.

They will help you to begin to feel a little differently about responding to adults when things don't feel right to you.

These reminders can also help you understand that your emotions and how you feel are important. Anyone, including adults, who say otherwise, are not correct.

I really hope these can help you or help someone that you know.

Much love, Lis

IMPORTANT REMINDERS FOR CHILDREN

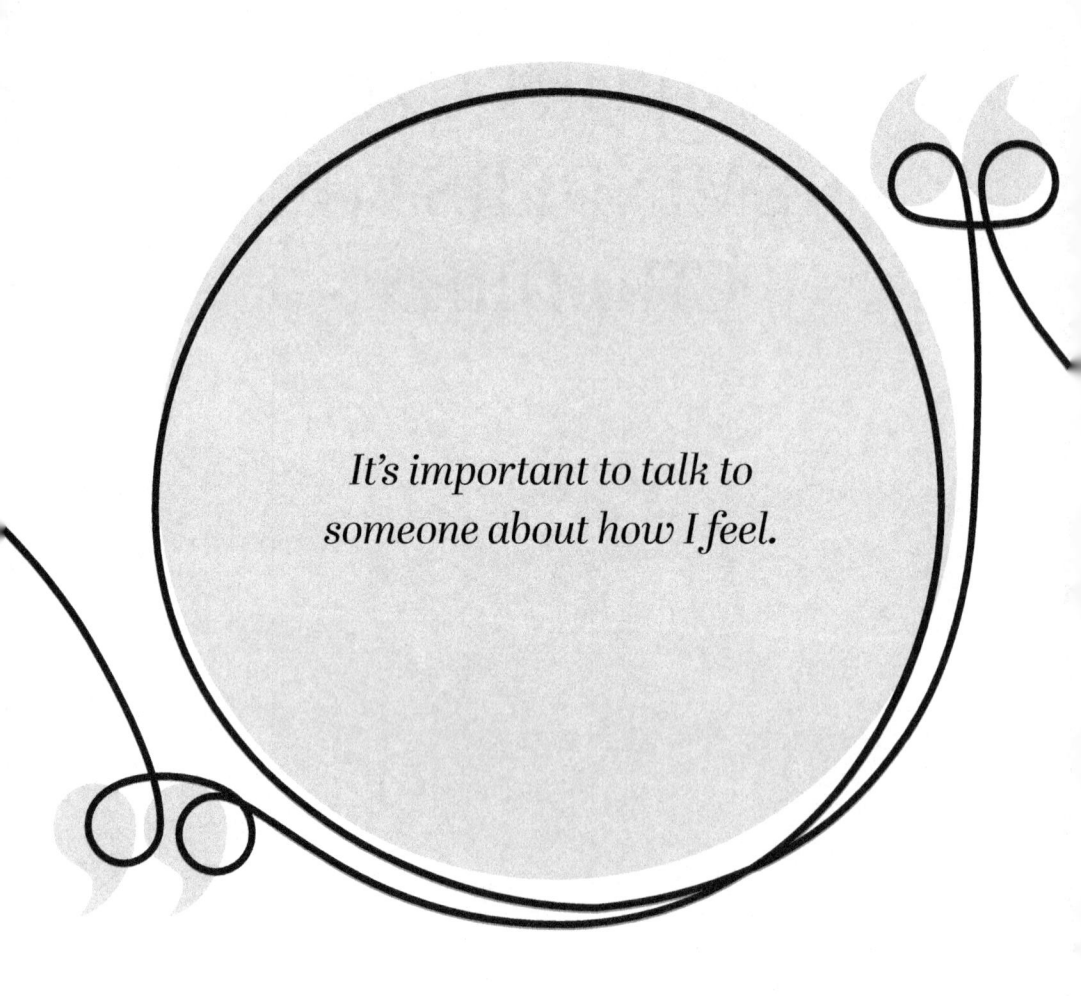

It's important to talk to someone about how I feel.

It's ok to feel sad sometimes.

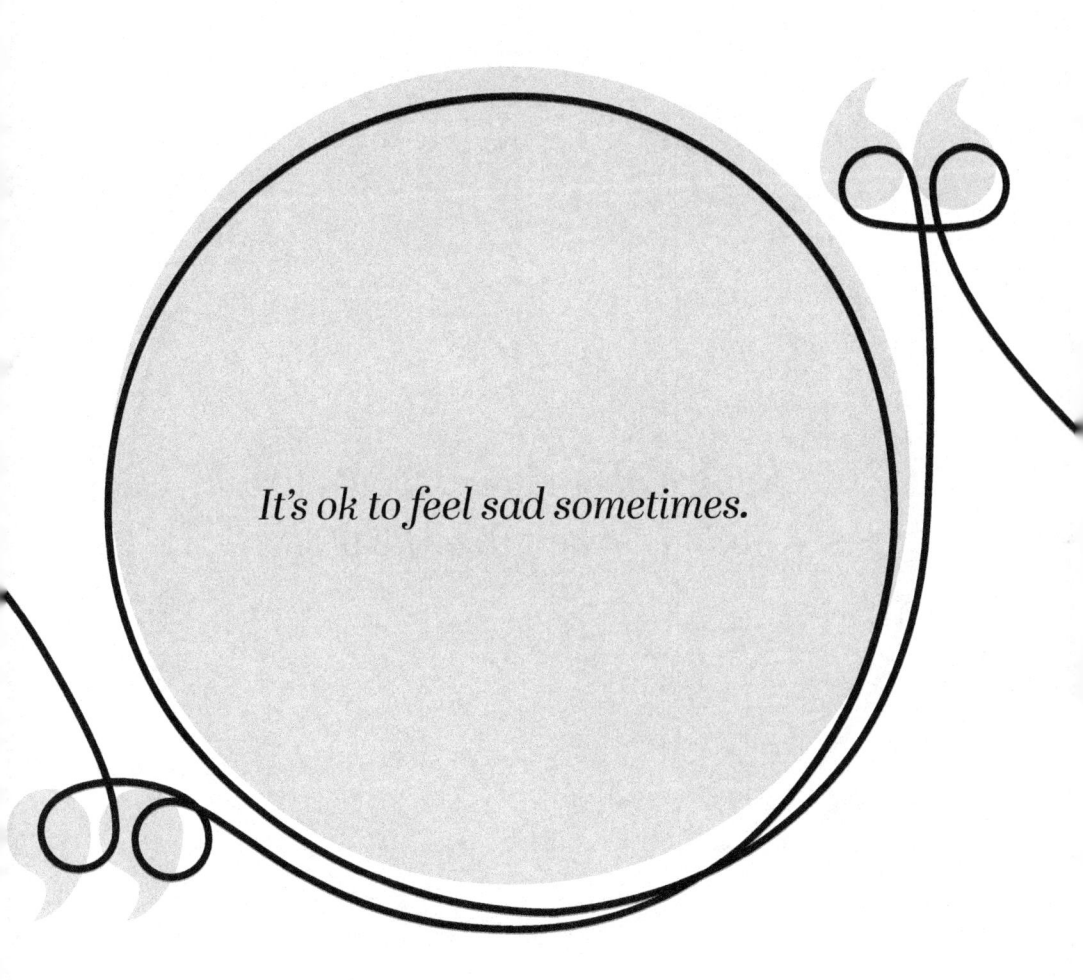

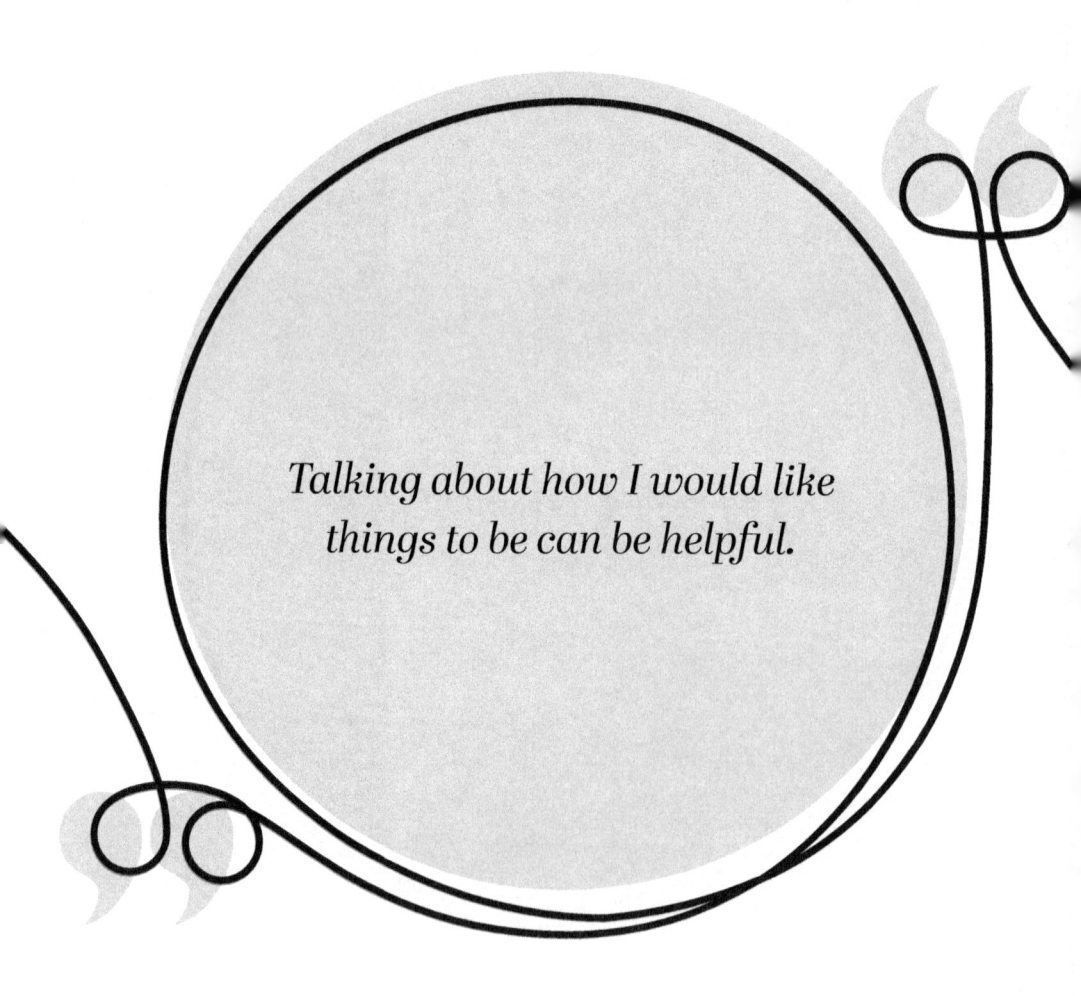

Talking about how I would like things to be can be helpful.

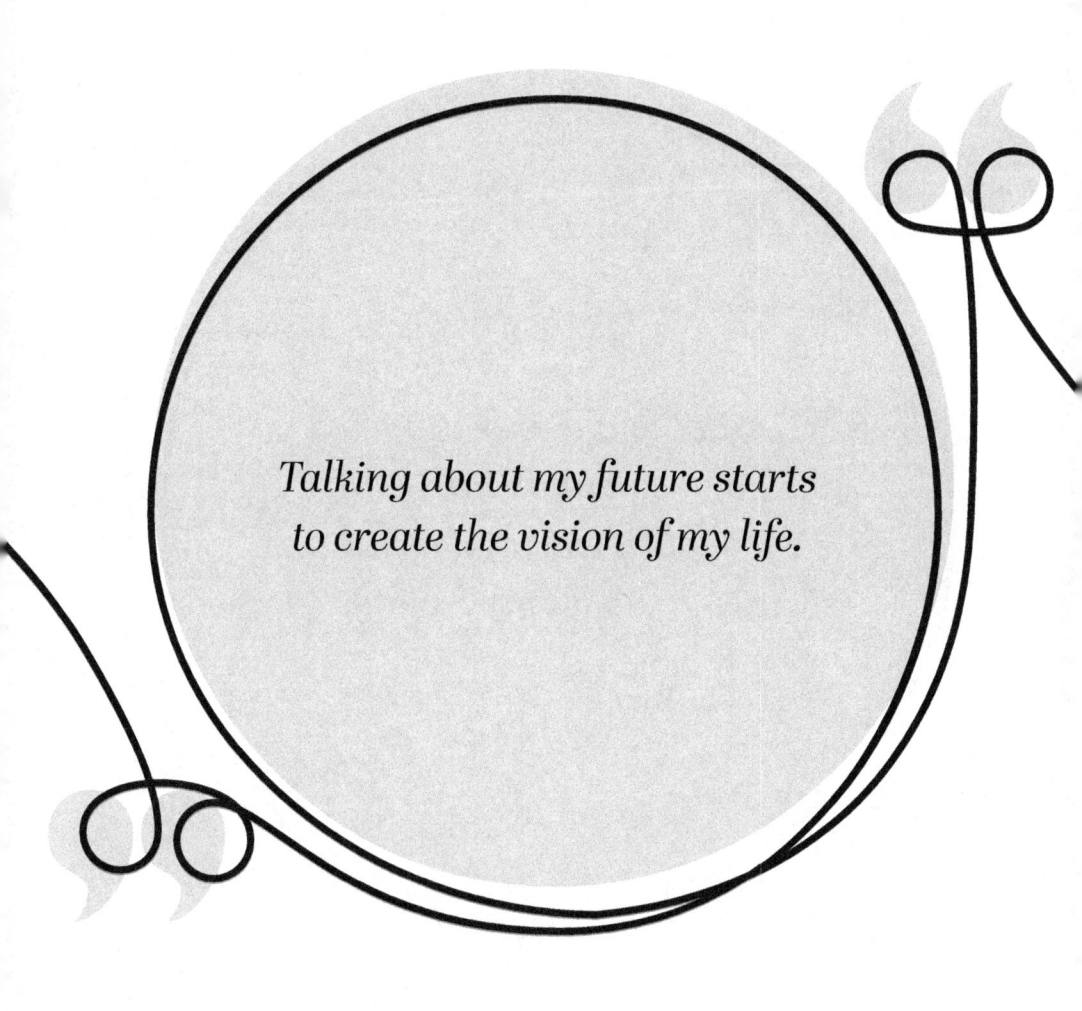

Talking about my future starts to create the vision of my life.

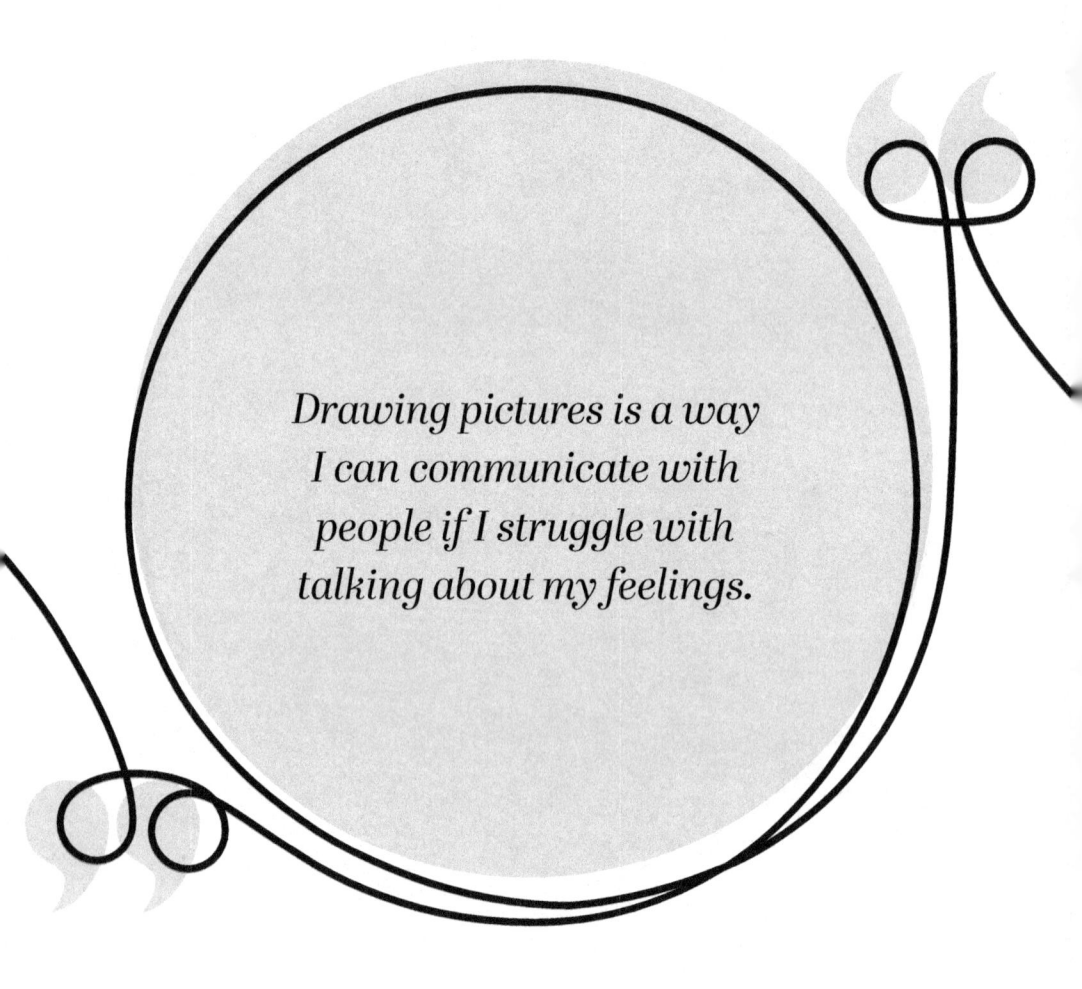

Drawing pictures is a way I can communicate with people if I struggle with talking about my feelings.

*I have full control over
my imagination.*

It's fun to imagine happy things.

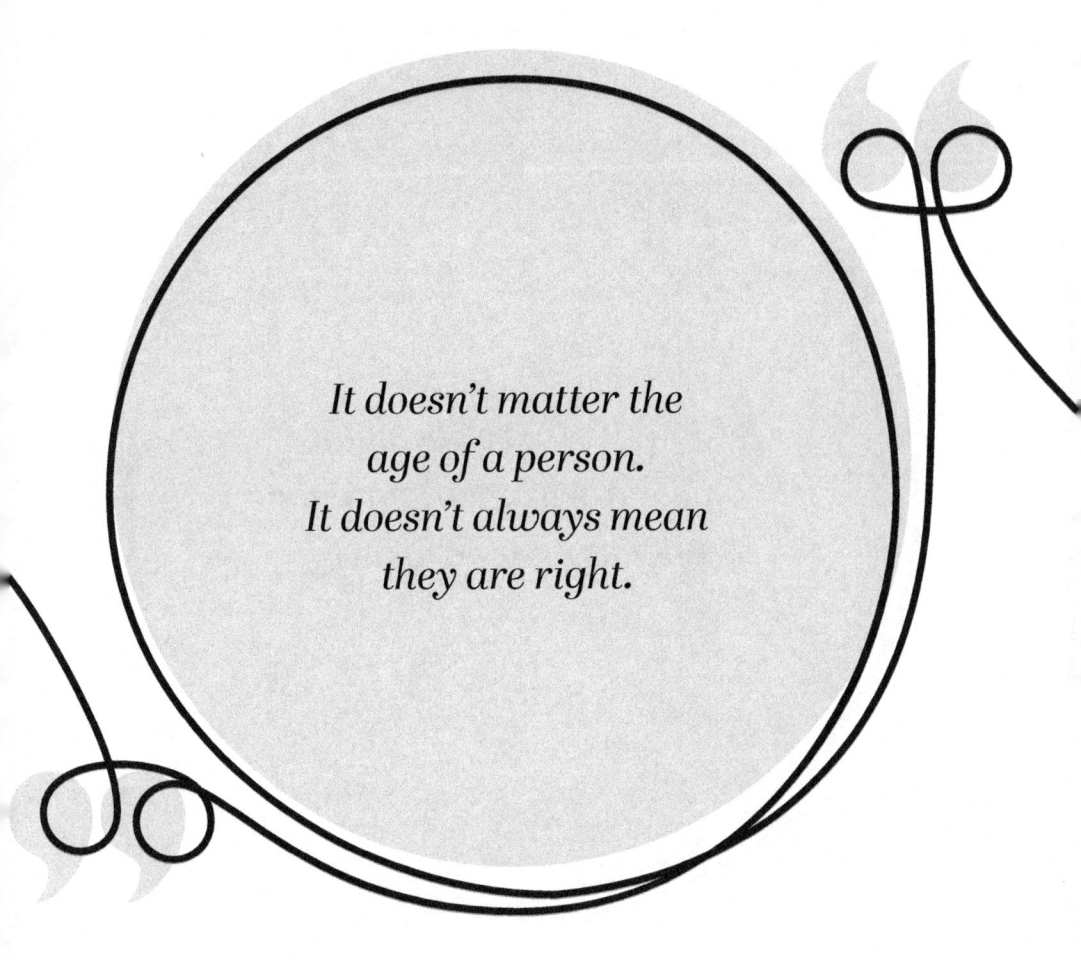

It doesn't matter the age of a person. It doesn't always mean they are right.

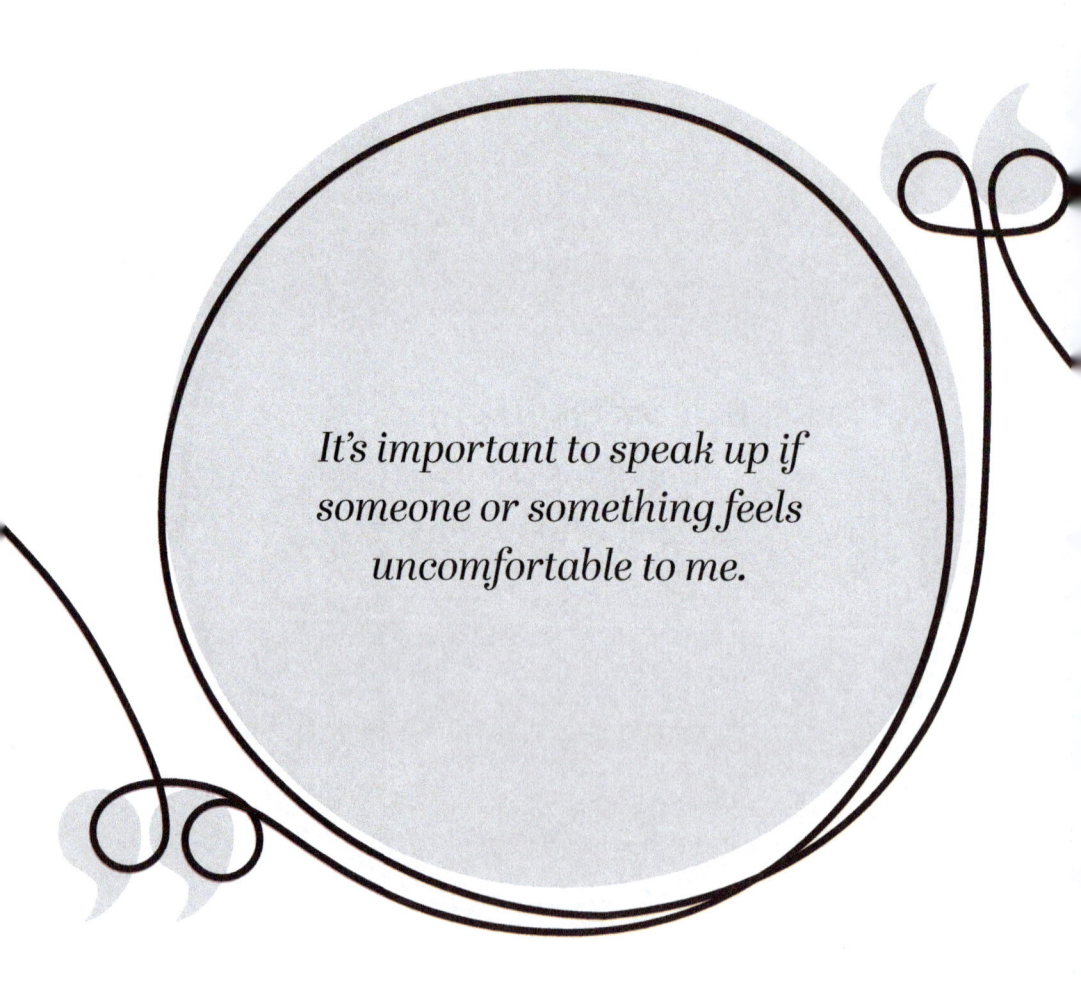

It's important to speak up if someone or something feels uncomfortable to me.

This includes family and parents.

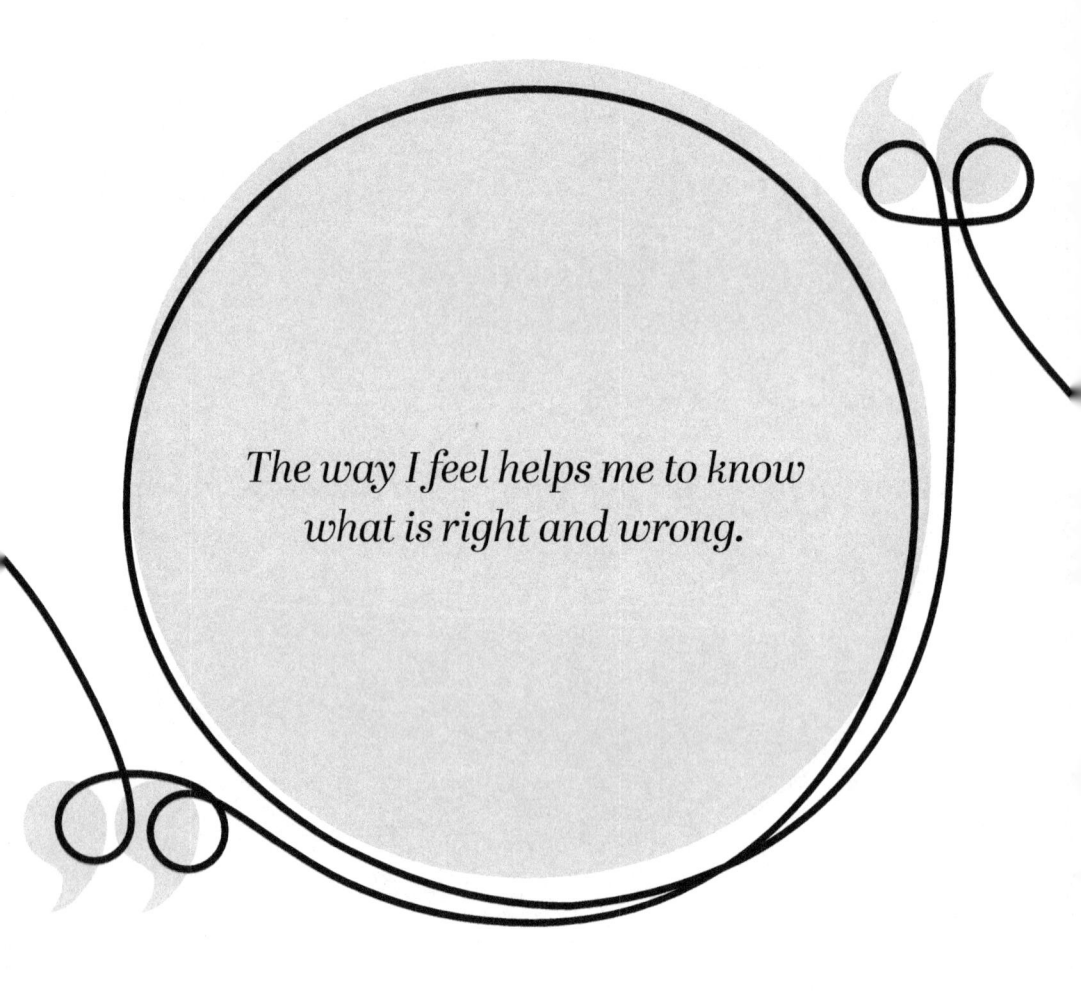

The way I feel helps me to know what is right and wrong.

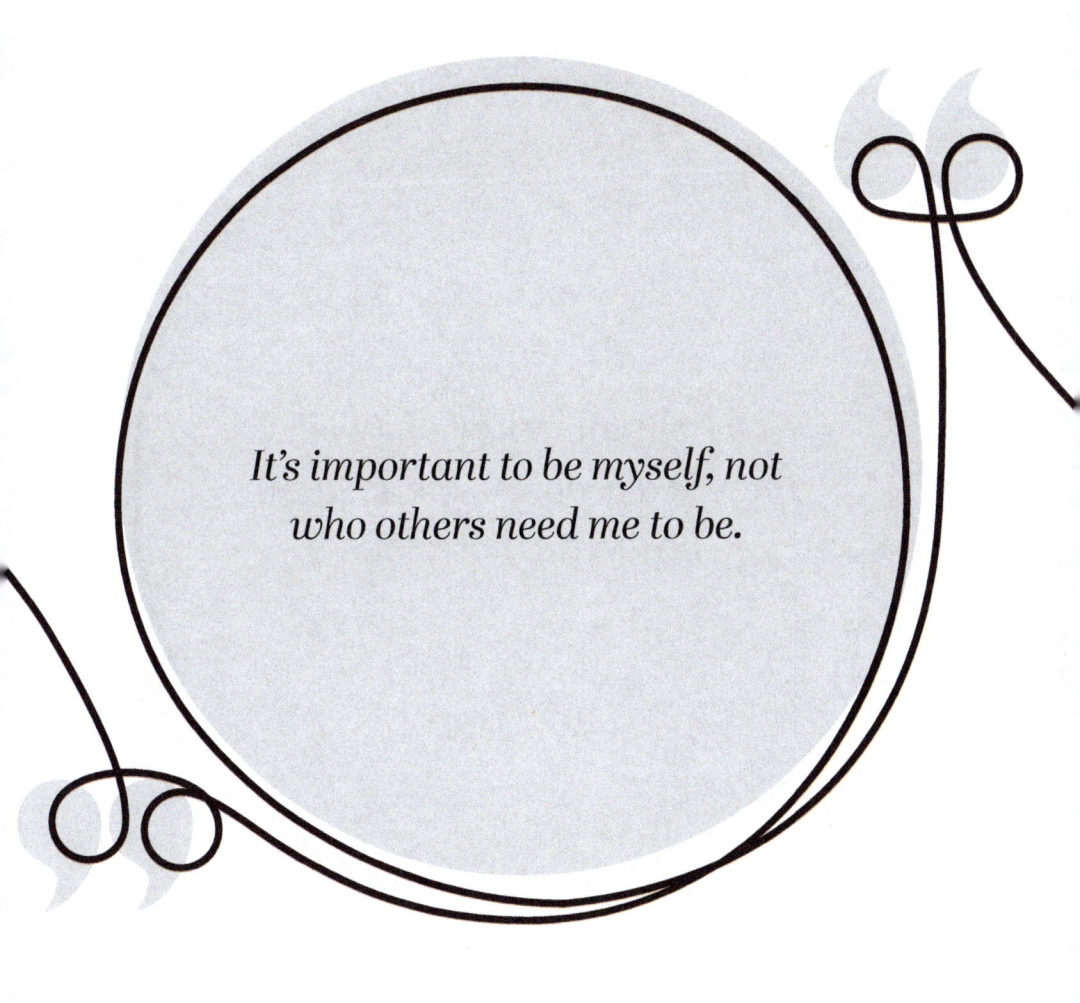

It's important to be myself, not who others need me to be.

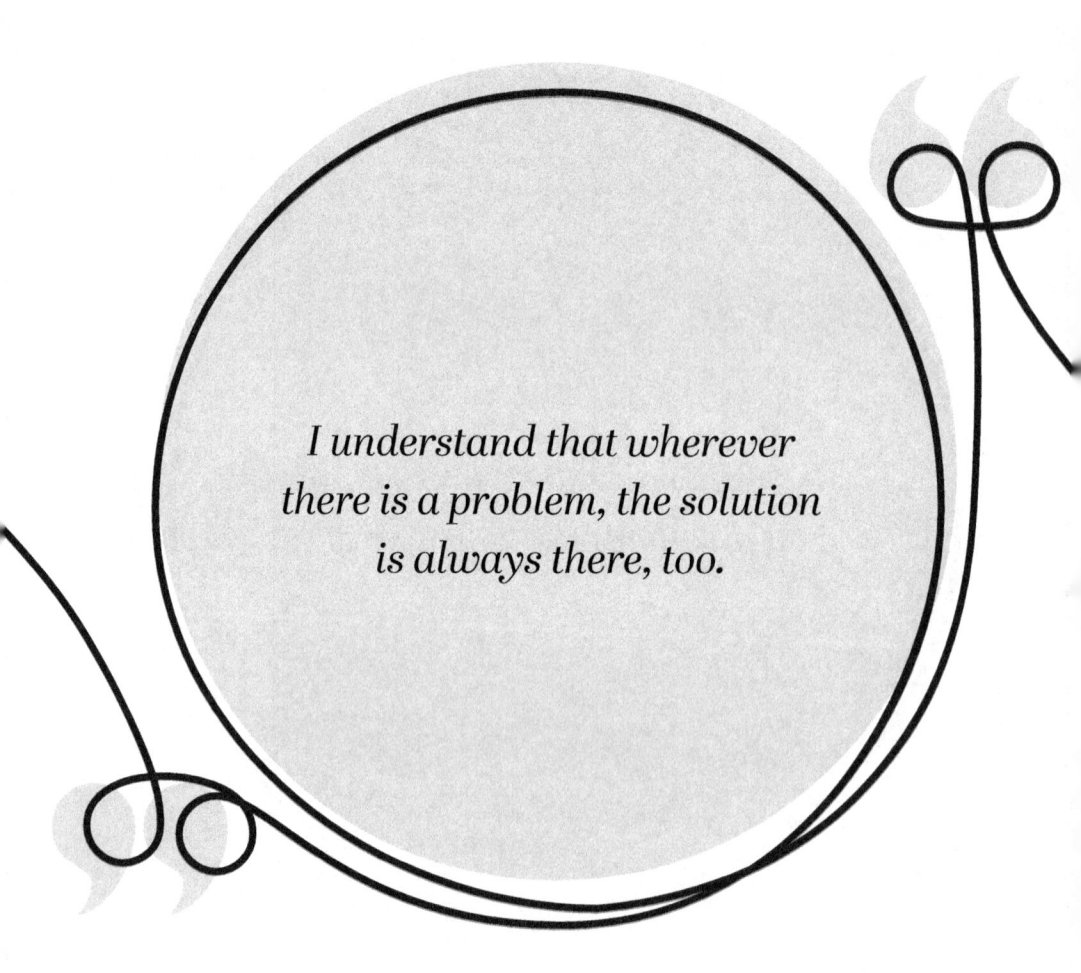

I understand that wherever there is a problem, the solution is always there, too.

I am optimistic about what's coming.

Day by day, I can be closer to my happy visions.

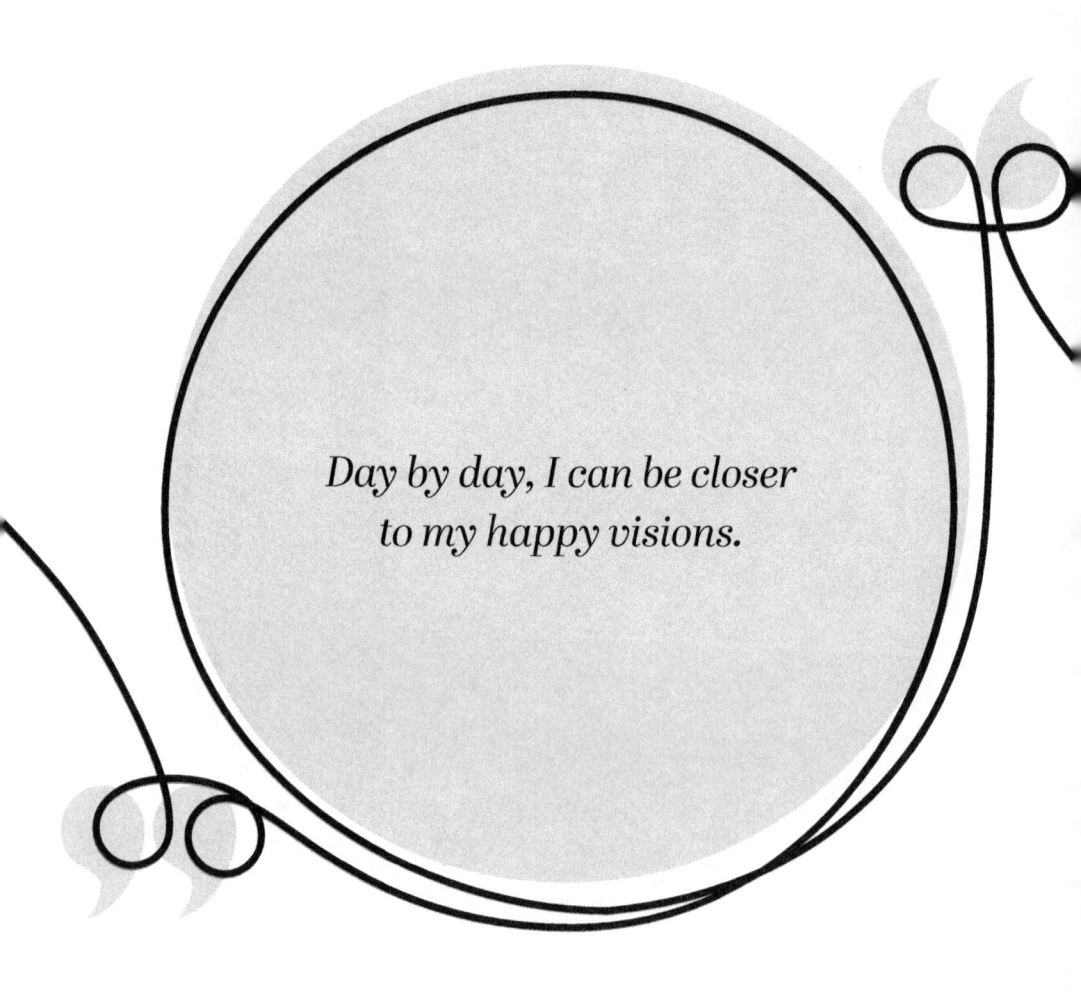

I deserve to be happy.

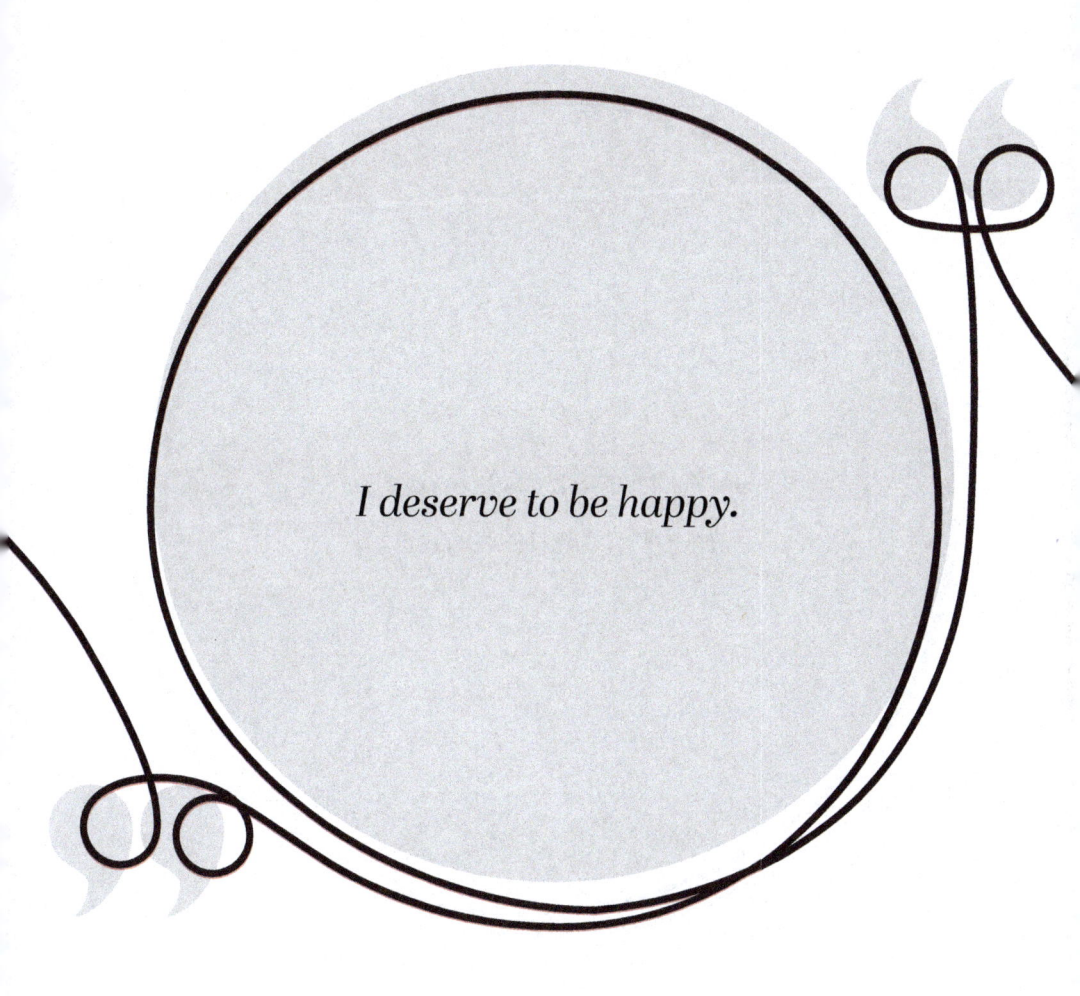

My experiences help me to grow and learn.

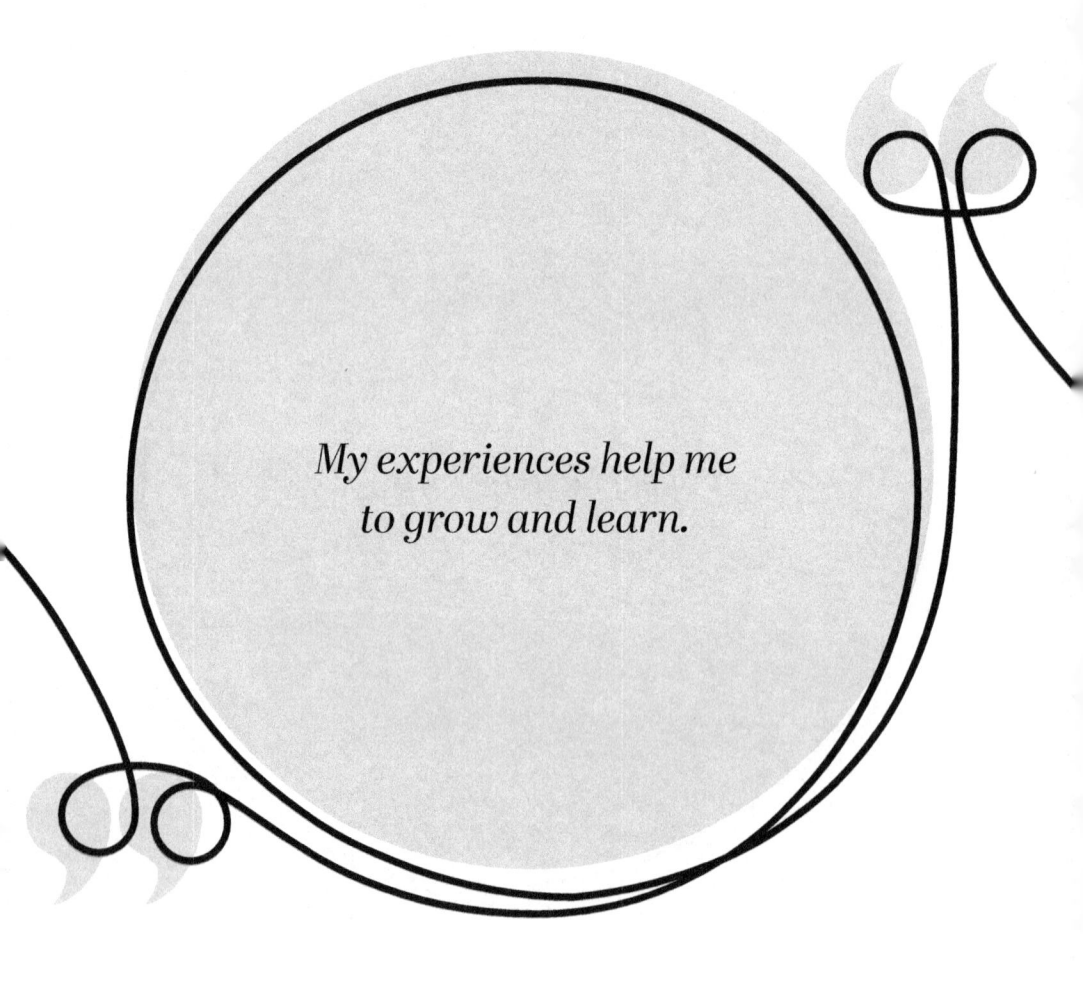

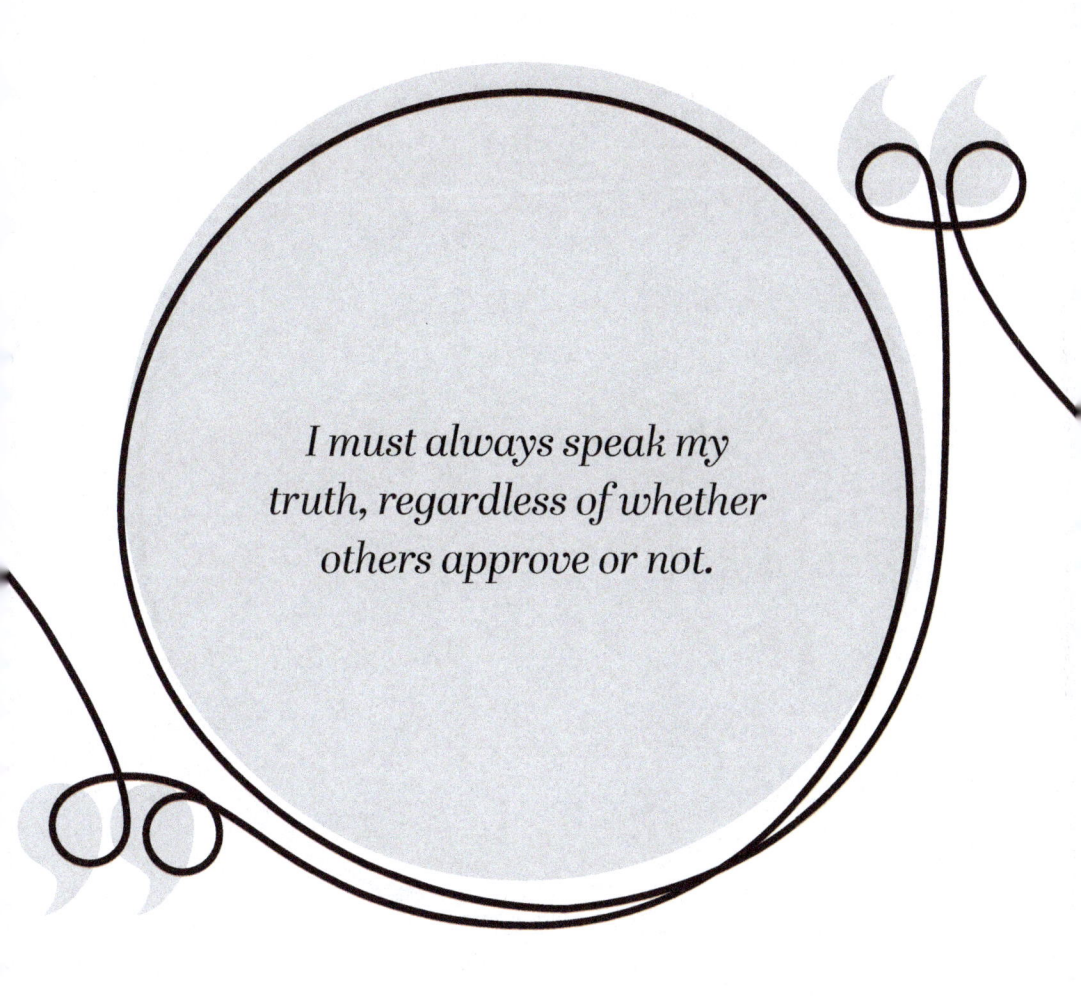

I must always speak my truth, regardless of whether others approve or not.

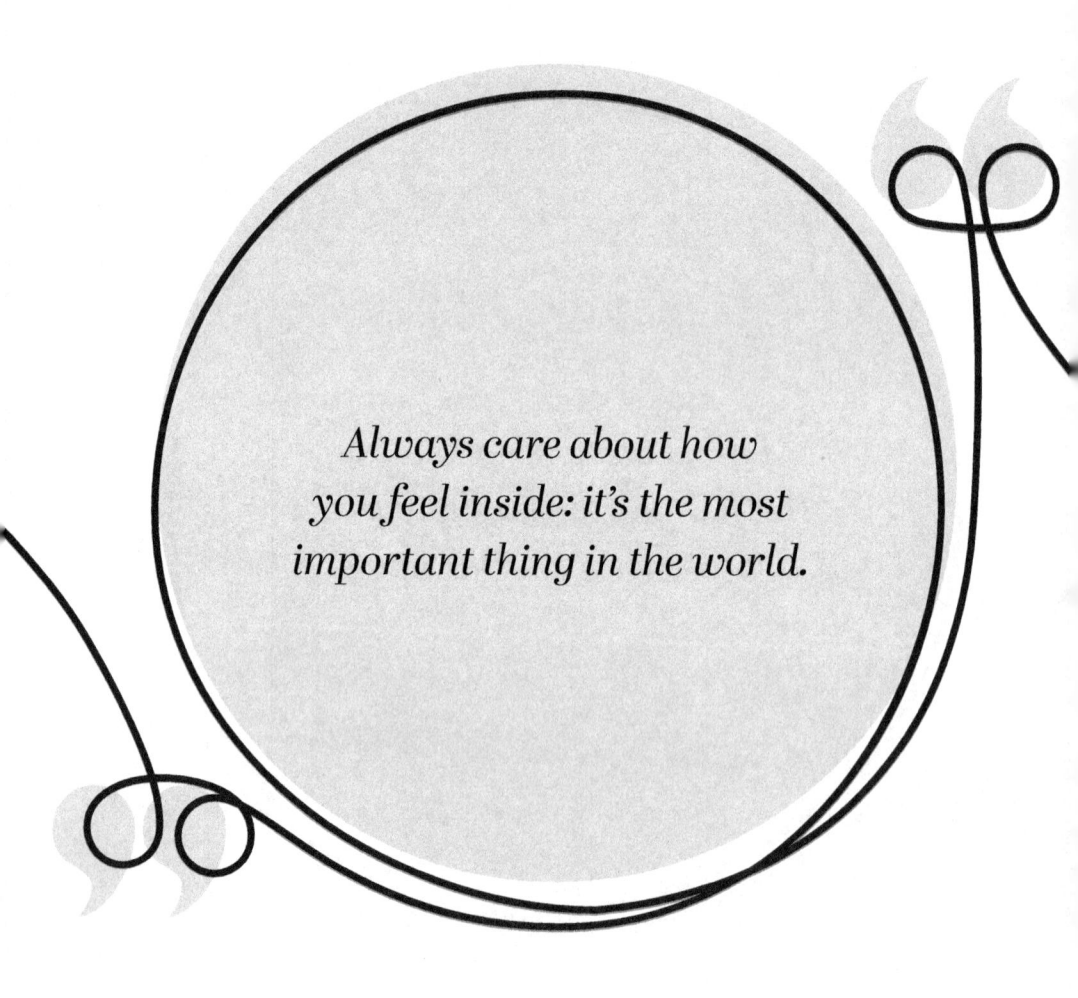

Always care about how you feel inside: it's the most important thing in the world.

*My feelings are valid.
My emotions are valid.*

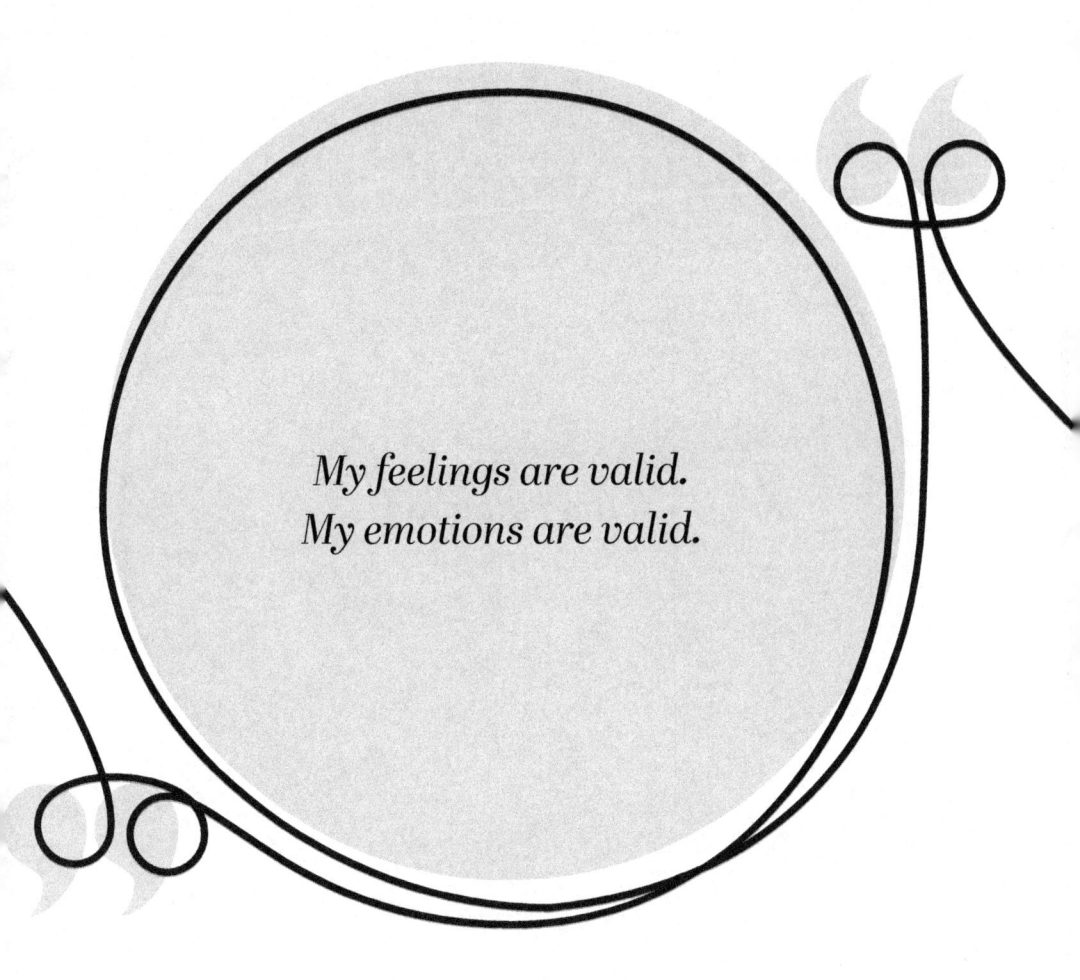

I am valuable.

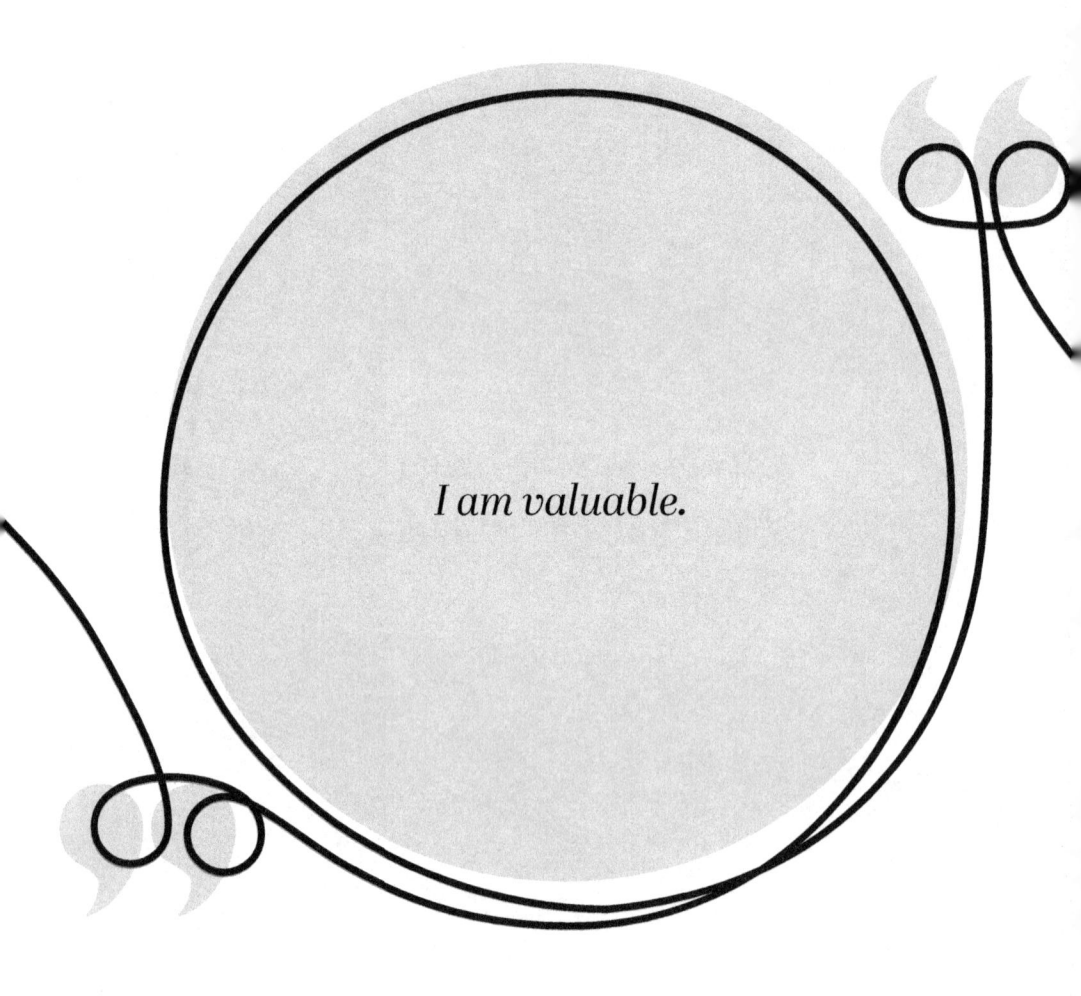

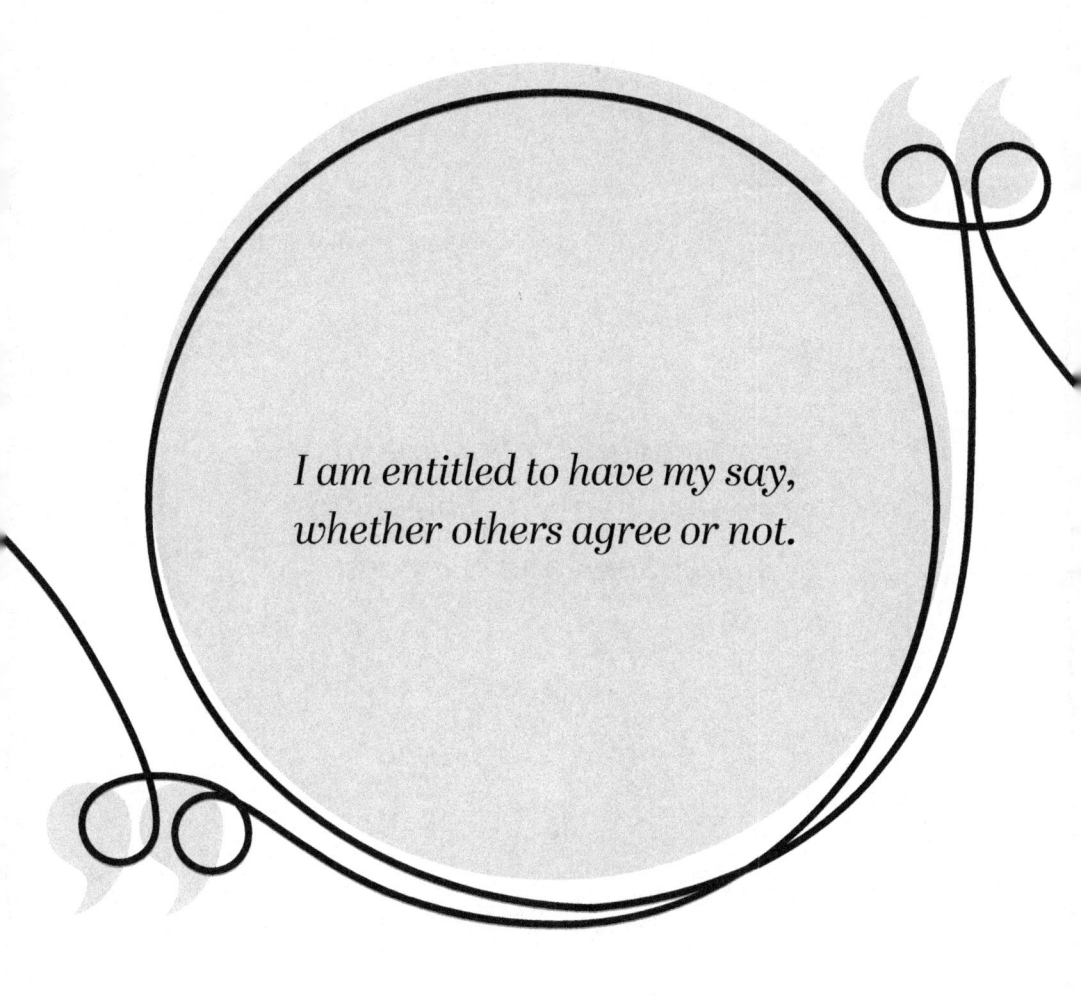

I am entitled to have my say, whether others agree or not.

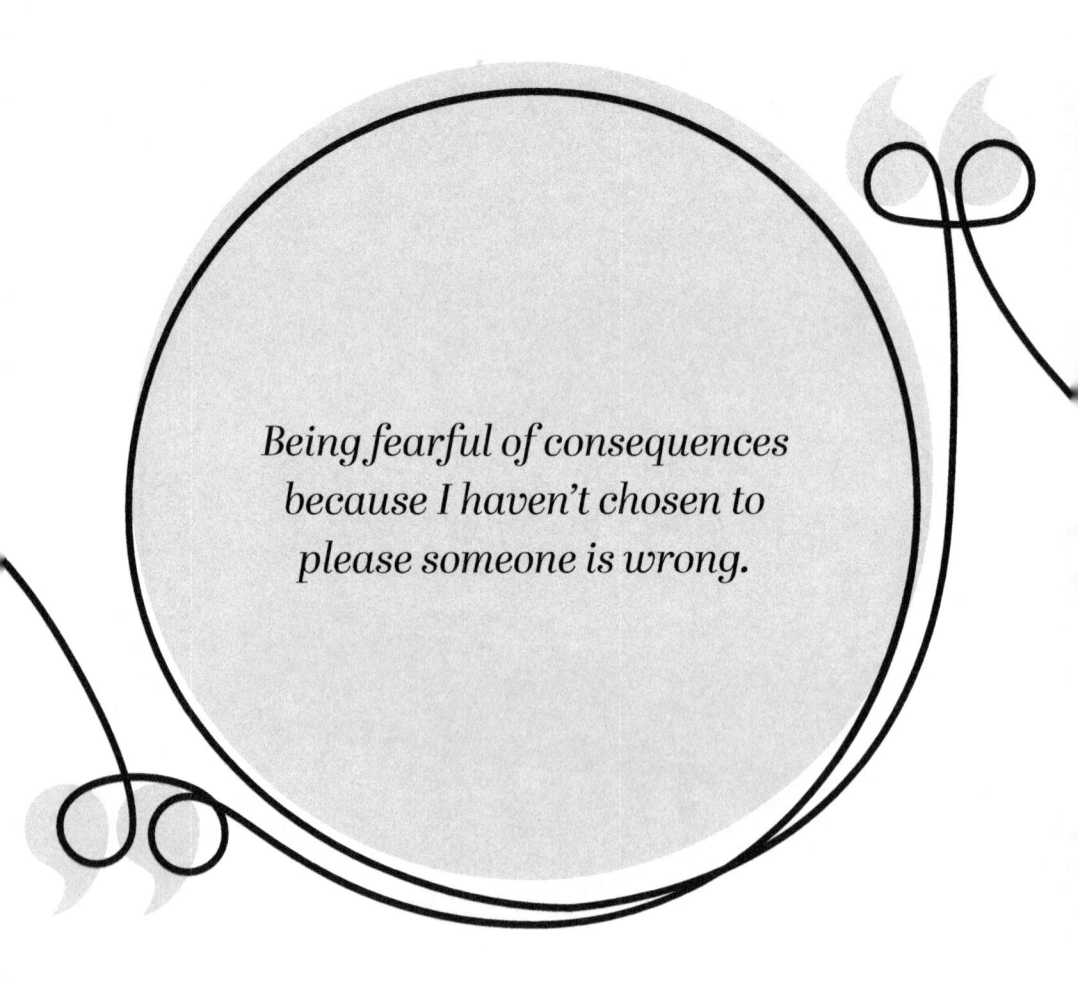

Being fearful of consequences because I haven't chosen to please someone is wrong.

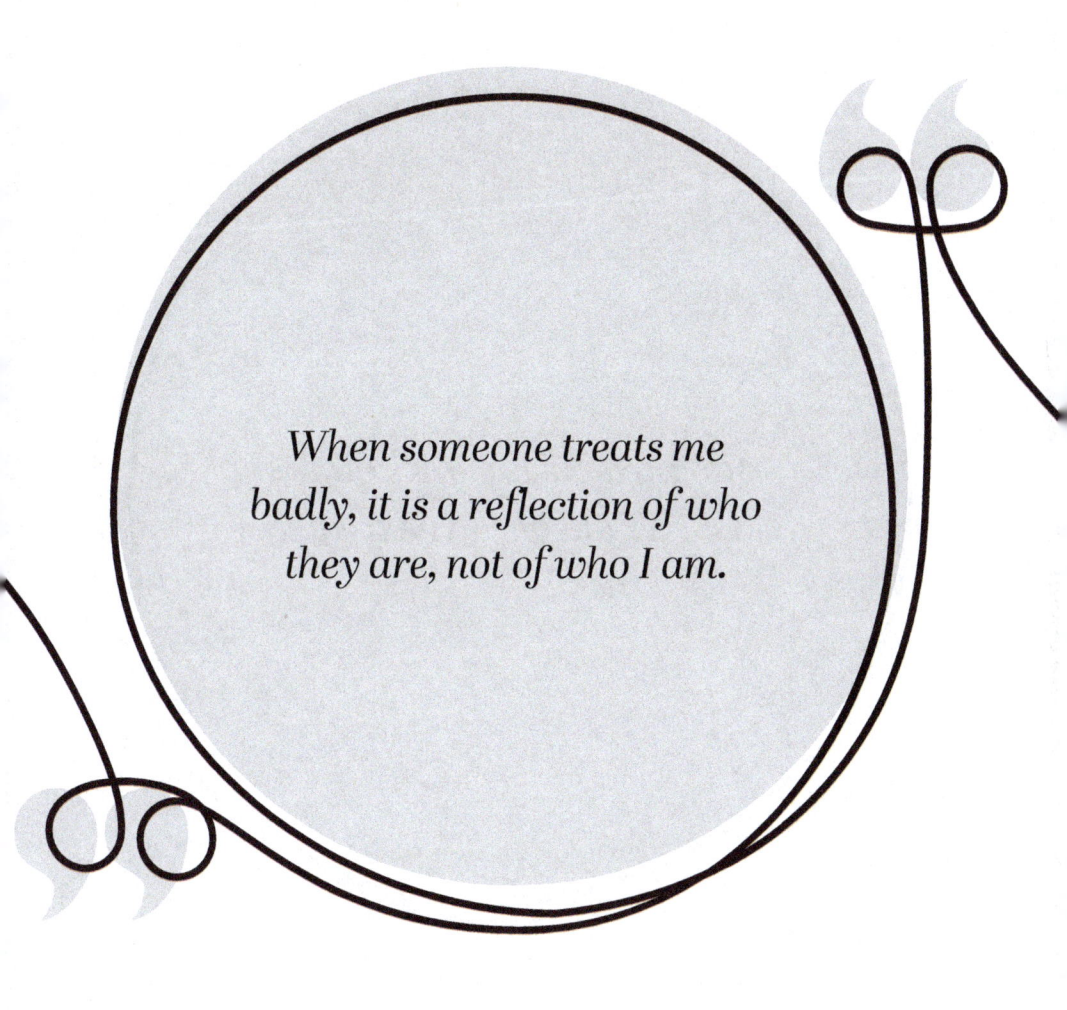

When someone treats me badly, it is a reflection of who they are, not of who I am.

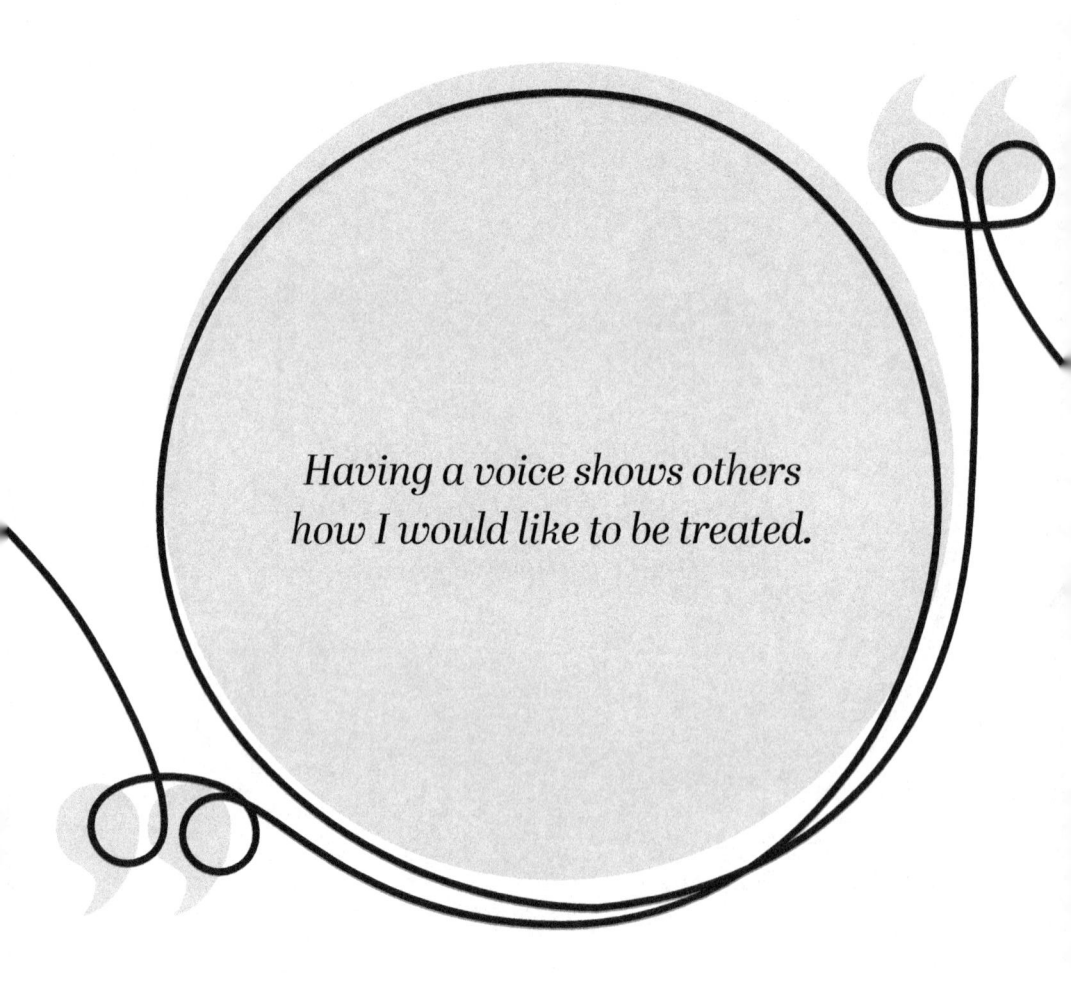

Having a voice shows others how I would like to be treated.

I am entitled to have choices that matter to me.

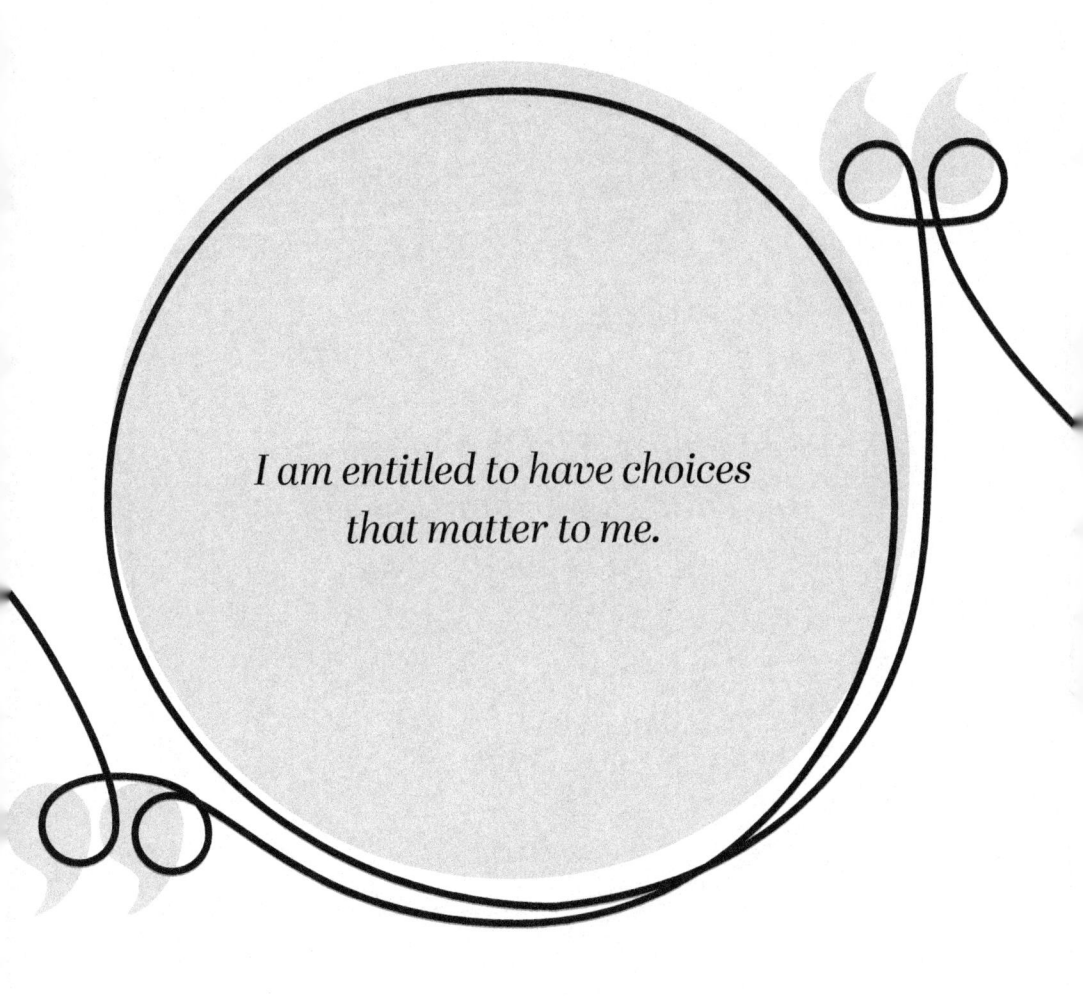

*Being a child doesn't mean
I don't know how I feel or
what is good for me.*

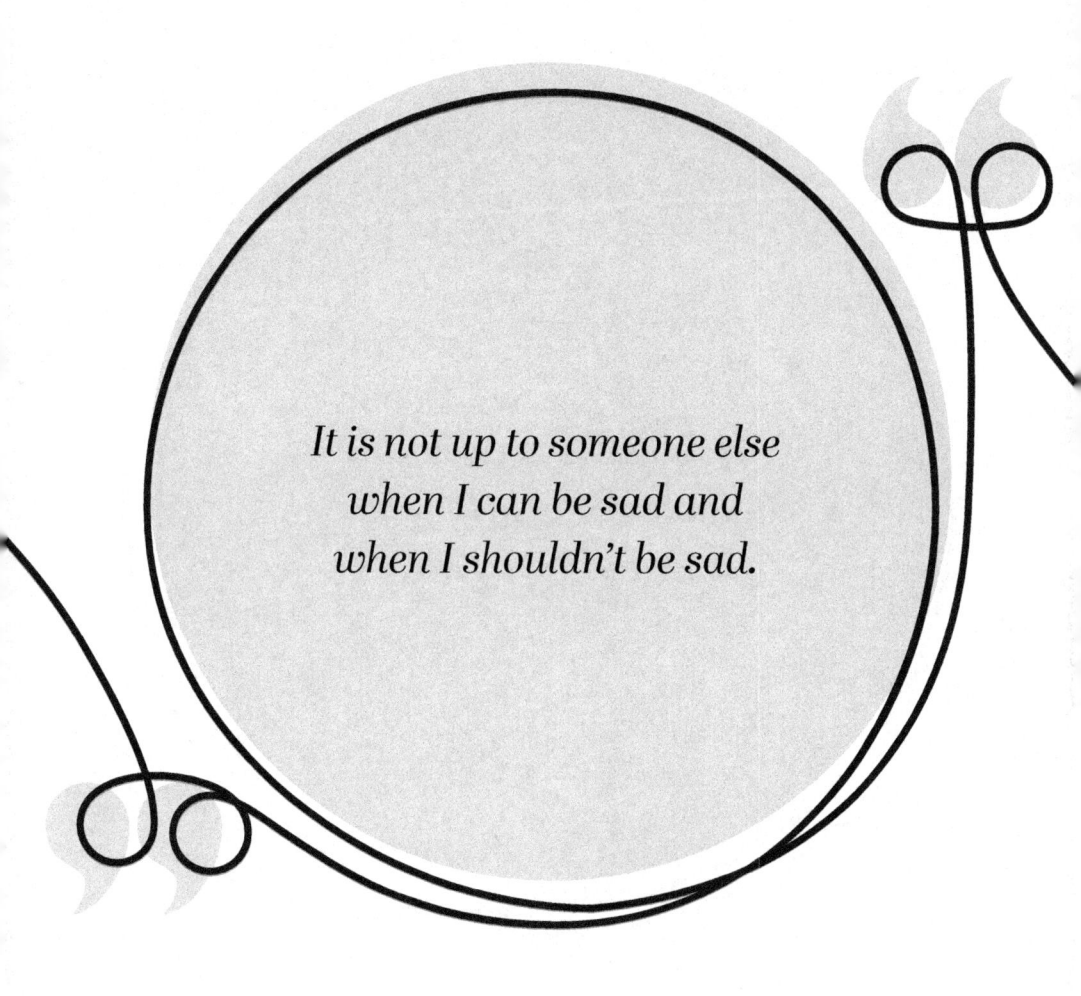

It is not up to someone else when I can be sad and when I shouldn't be sad.

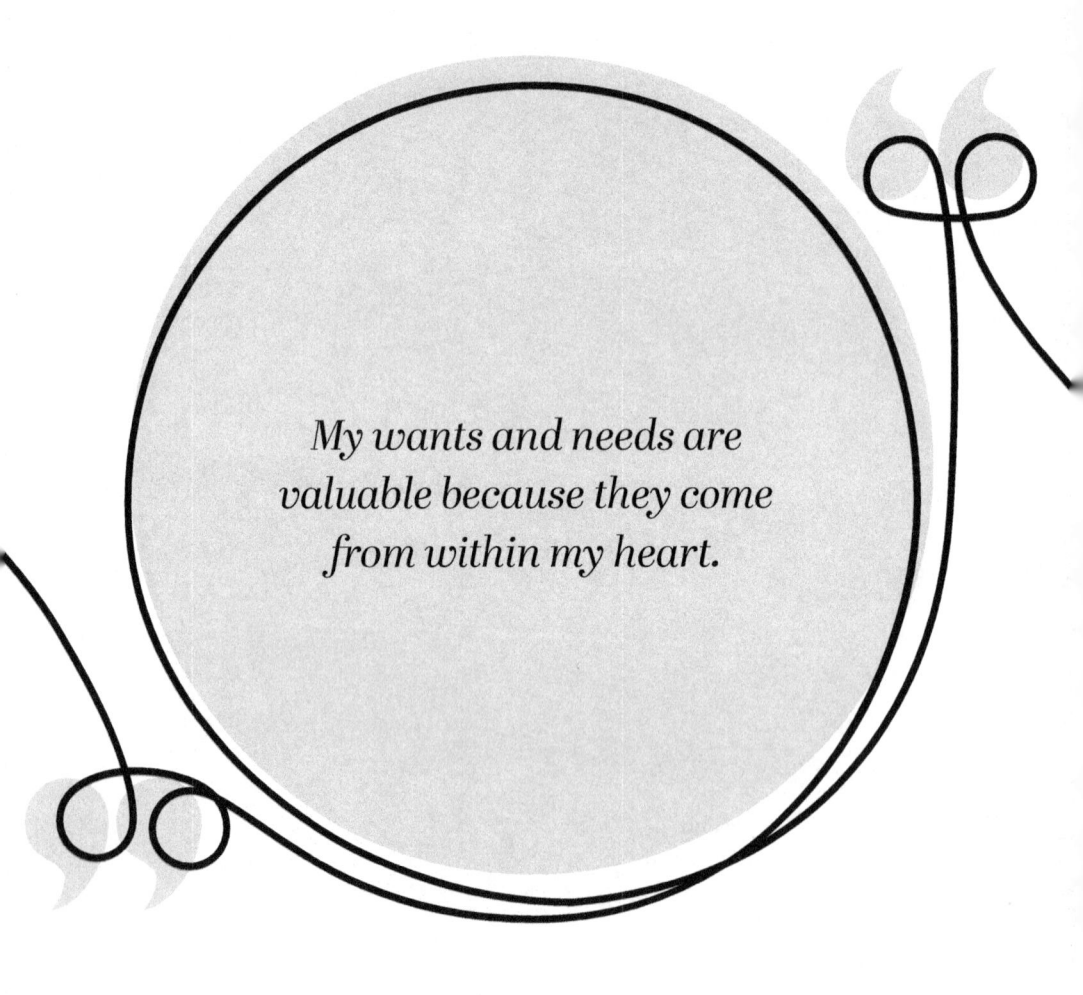

My wants and needs are valuable because they come from within my heart.

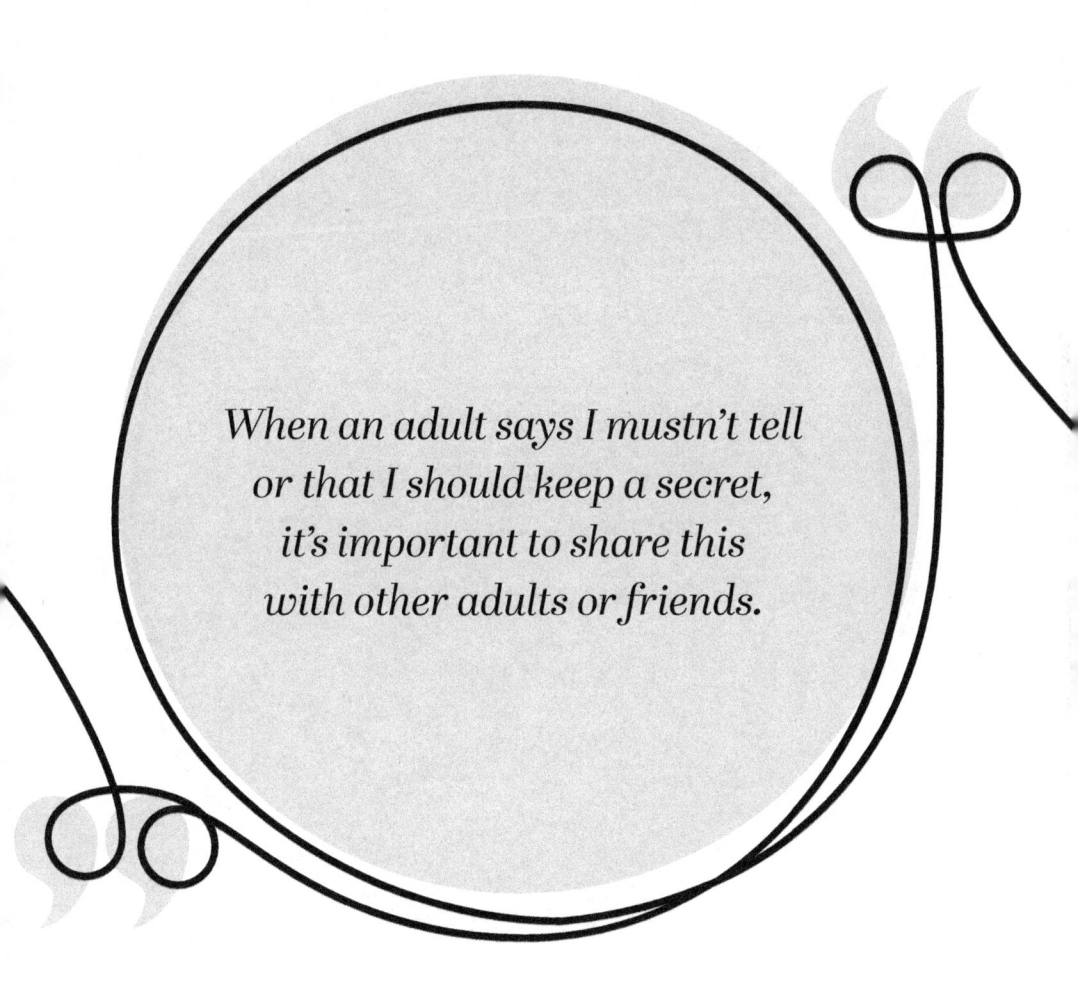

*When an adult says I mustn't tell
or that I should keep a secret,
it's important to share this
with other adults or friends.*

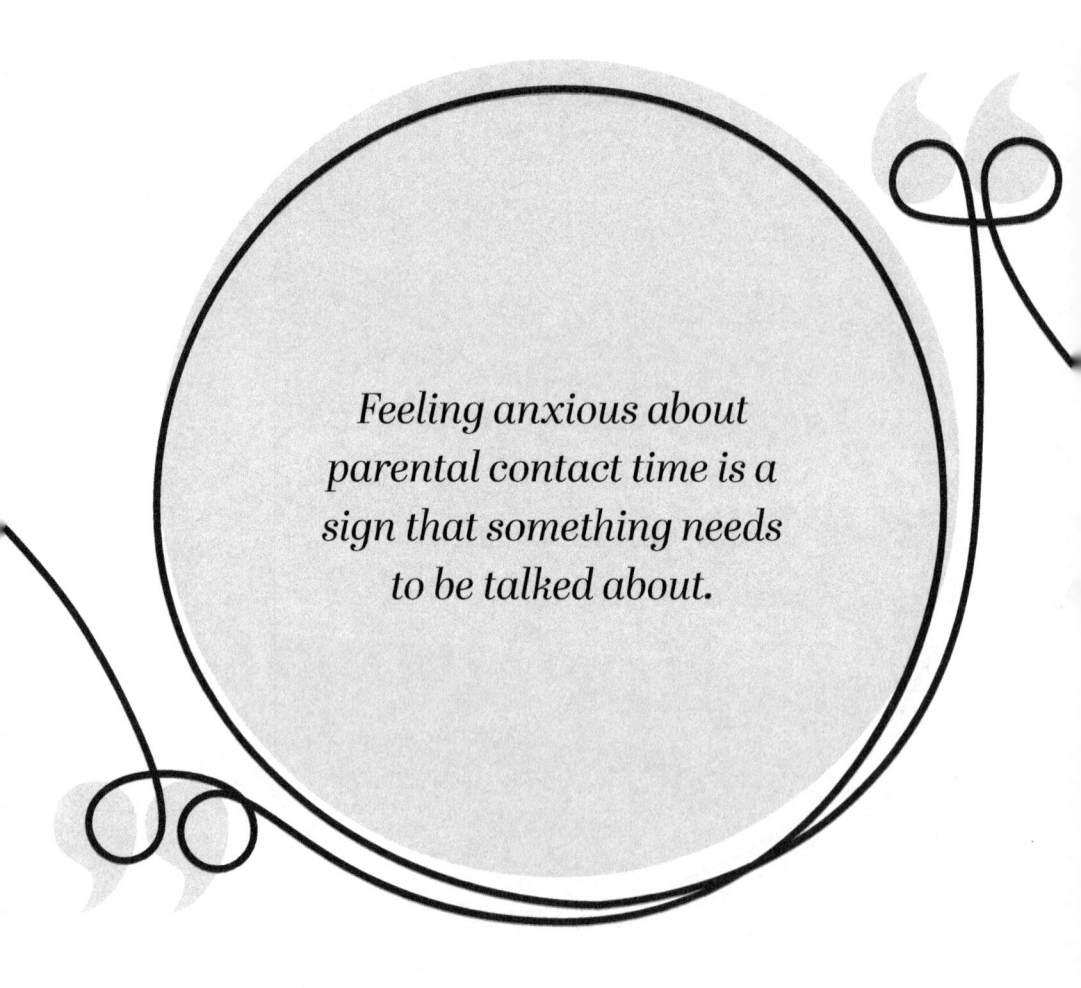

Feeling anxious about parental contact time is a sign that something needs to be talked about.

Loving someone doesn't mean its ok for them to treat me badly.

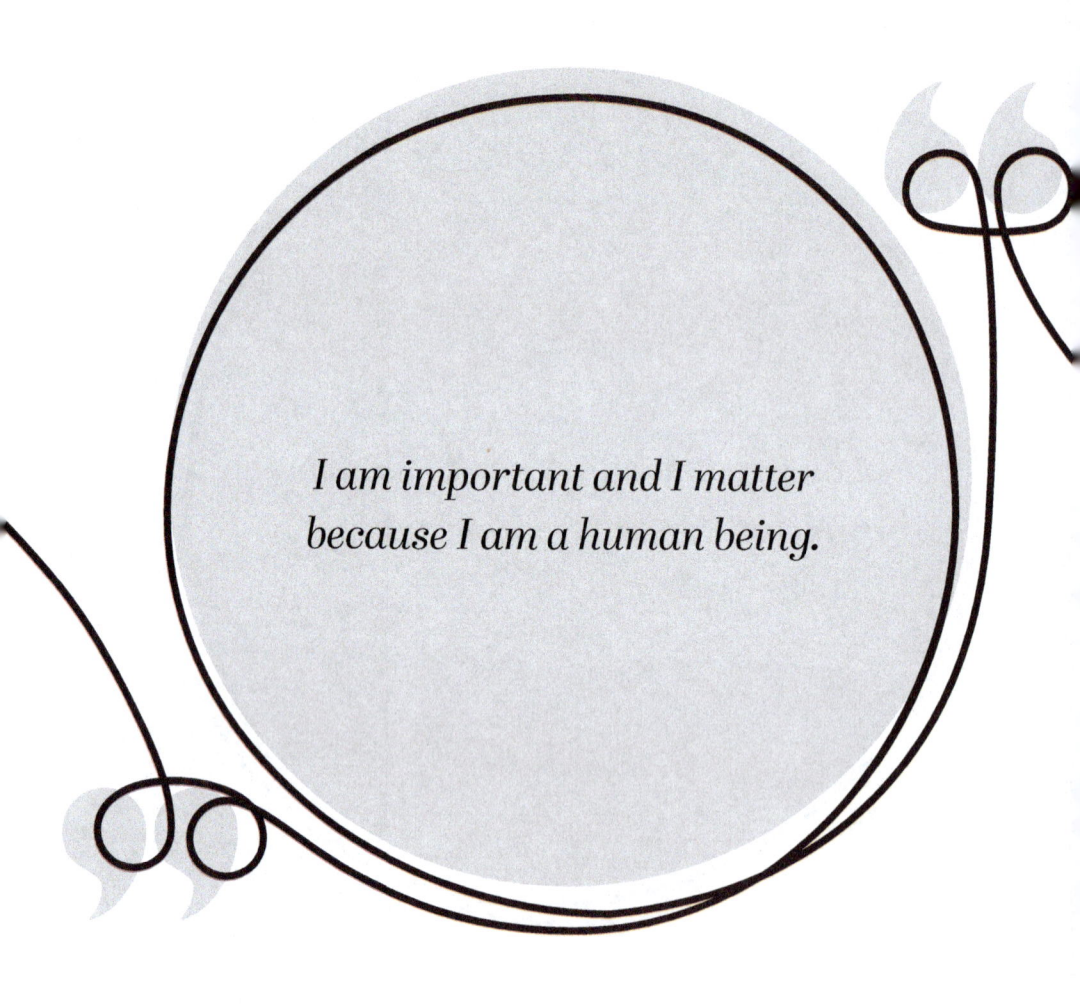

I am important and I matter because I am a human being.

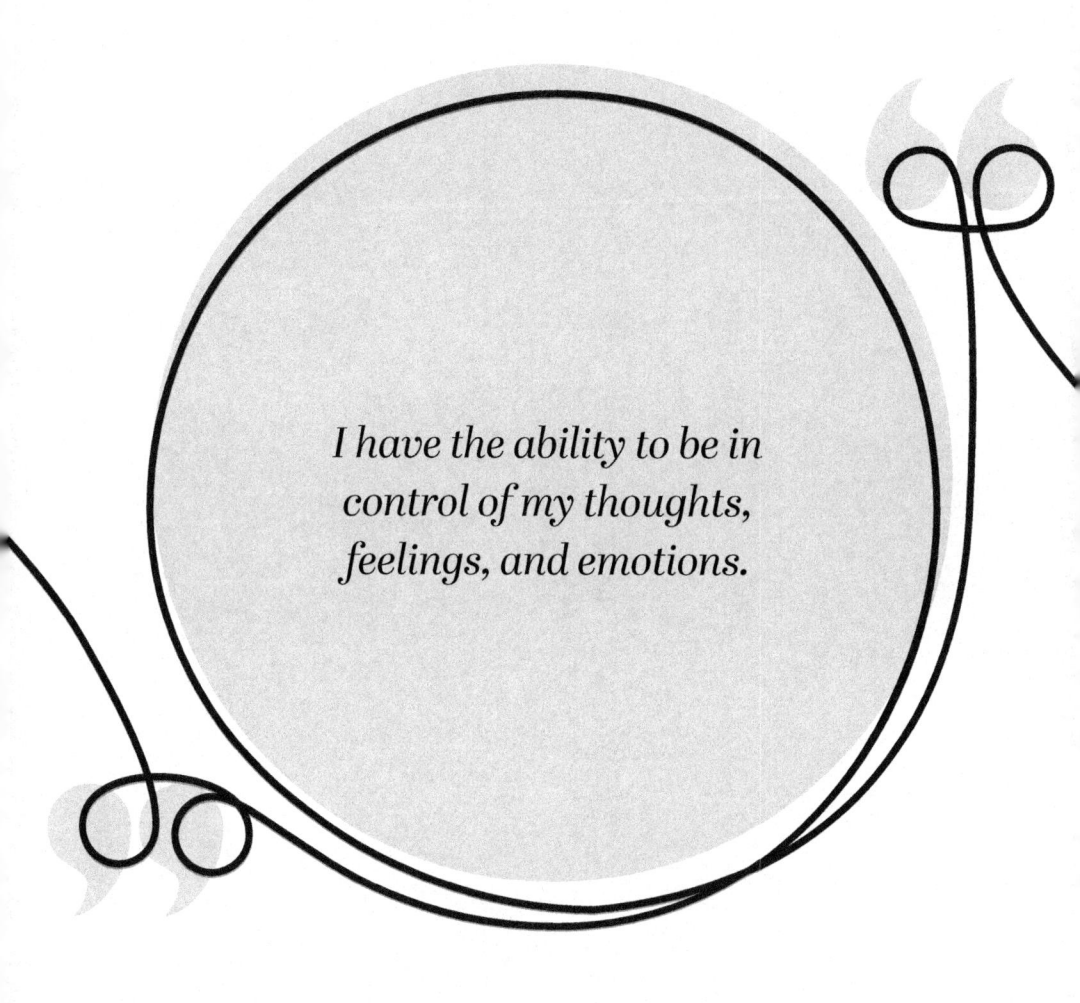

I have the ability to be in control of my thoughts, feelings, and emotions.

Write your own positive affirmation
I am

A Message to Your Child – Part 2

As children, you all have amazing hearts and should have wonderful visions for your future.

As you may be aware by now, my name is Lis Hoyte and helping and supporting children is very important to me. It is so important that you begin to understand that your voice is your magic wand. It can help to change your future and help you feel better about how you feel inside. It also encourages you to have confidence and to know that your feelings have value.

It is important for you to express to adults – whether in the home or out of the home – how you feel about your life and the people in your life. Remember that you are important, your feelings matter, and how you feel is a reflection of the life you are living right here and now.

The stories I have included in this guide should help you and your parents to respond to adults when something feels wrong to you. You must be able to speak out, say how something makes you feel, and question whether it is something that you should be involved in as a child.

Also remember that you should be living your life, not feeling responsible for any adult's feelings. They are the adult's feelings to own, not yours.

Stay curious and blessed and look after your heart. Childhood is meant to be fun, stress-free and enjoyable. If anything is stopping that from happening in your life, speak to someone you trust.

Dance on! Much love, Lis xx

Final Word to Parents

Support your children and yourself by making decisions that will create peace in your hearts.

Review Ask

Thank you for reading this book and I hope that you found it useful. Love this book? Don't forget to leave a review! Thank you so much.

Get in touch with Lis:

https://www.facebook.com/lis.hoyte.315
http://linkedin.com/in/lis-hoyte-892ab31a6
https://www.lisreallywhat.com
https://calendly.com/lisreallywhat/15min
www.lishoyte.com
www.lisreallywhat.com

Craving more?

Wow, this book is beautifully written with such passion and determination. I have already recommended it to friends who are or are in coercive relationships. But even as a guide to help change your mindset, it's worth a read. Absolute pleasure to read, thank you Lis

Amazon Review

About the Author

Lis Hoyte is the founder and CEO of Lis, Really? What? Coaching and Speaking LTD. Lis Hoyte is an author, facilitator of the VOICE Programme, certified speaker, life coach (empowering women and men to break free from coercive, controlling relationships), specialist consultant in coercive control, domestic abuse advocate (especially for the voice of the child), and a survivor.

Lis started her career as a youth support worker, working with disabled young people, helping them to access and be a part of social activities. Lis also focused her attention on supporting young people with emotional and behavioural difficulties who resided in independent children's homes. From this, Lis then started her career teaching in both mainstream and independent schools, covering both KS3 and KS4 at GCSE, specialising in Humanities, Health and Social Care and Psychology.

Lis is the author of "Break Free" (2021), which maps Lis' transformational journey and paradigm shift out of a coercive, controlling relationship that spanned nearly two decades. Lis's purpose is to spread awareness of coercive control and to support others experiencing this type of abuse. Lis has planned curricula for schools to offer students and teachers support in understanding the prevalence of coercive control.

Lis' focus is on the importance of the Inner Game for self-healing and empowerment. Lis' "Break Free" programme has helped many men and women to break free from their abusive relationships.

Lis holds a Diploma in Life Coaching, BA Honours in Sociology and Criminology, and an MSc in Crime and Community Safety Evidence-Based Practice (EBP).

NOTES

NOTES

NOTES

NOTES

NOTES

NOTES

NOTES

NOTES

NOTES

NOTES

NOTES

NOTES

NOTES

NOTES

Printed in Great Britain
by Amazon